Advance Praise for *It's Hard Being You*

"Finally, here is a story about disability told by a person *with* a disability. Emery doesn't sugarcoat the losses and limits, but also gives us rare insights into real life with disability, including lessons learned, joy, and even humor. Her memoir is an eye-opener about the barriers our ableist culture—including our own fumbling interactions with people with disabilities—creates. And how we can all live better."

THERESA METZMAKER, executive director/CEO
of the Michigan Disability Rights Coalition

"Sharon's story is searing, poignant, funny, touching. It is a tale told with the bark on, as the saying goes. A story about those two most fundamental elements, life and death. And how life goes on, even after death stops to knock on your door. A resilient story, told by a brave and remarkable woman."

JOHN ENGLER, governor of Michigan, 1991-2003

"Journalist Sharon Emery dishes up a rich, powerful, and beautifully written memoir about parenting a child with special needs and surviving the loss of that child, the complicated deaths of her siblings, and the personal and professional challenges presented by a lifelong stutter that helped drive the author's career success. This is an engrossing and unflinching read."

JUDY WINTER, author of *Breakthrough Parenting for Children with Special Needs: Raising the Bar of Expectations*

It's Hard Being You

Readers are encouraged to go to www.MissionPointPress.com to contact the author or to find information on how to buy this book in bulk at a discounted rate.

Published by Mission Point Press
2554 Chandler Rd.
Traverse City, MI 49696
(231) 421-9513
MissionPointPress.com

To connect with the author, visit www.sharon-emery.com

Cover design by Ben Schneider
Book design by Heather Lee Shaw

Hardcover ISBN: 978-1-954786-55-4
Softcover ISBN: 978-1-954786-56-1
Library of Congress Control Number: 2021919403

Printed in the United States of America

IT'S HARD

HARD

A Primer on Being Happy Anyway

BEING

YOU

Sharon Emery

MISSION POINT PRESS

To my children, Justin, Benjamin and Caitlin ... and to all those struggling to figure out if the losses we suffer and the limits we encounter come to any good.

Dear, Family
I Sorry Sympathy
I miss you
Jessica
john &sharon, justin,ben ,caitlin
GoodBye

Table of Contents

Foreword

Oh, there's a river that winds on forever,
I'm gonna see where it leads.
Oh, there's a mountain that no man has mounted,
I'm gonna stand on the peak.

Those opening lyrics to Lord Huron's song "Ends of the Earth" resonated with me as soon as I heard them in 2012, when the band's debut album "Lonesome Dreams" was released. I had been diagnosed with ALS just the previous year, and the song's expression of joy and determination to finish the journey, despite the challenges, really spoke to me. Having spent six years in the National Football League, as a safety with the News Orleans Saints, I needed that inspiration. My new journey would be very different from the one I had planned.

Not long after, the band was performing in New Orleans, where I live, and a friend reached out to see if they would play a concert at my home. They agreed. With friends and family gathered around, we became part of Lord Huron's music and they became part of our lives.

I was able to spend time that night talking with the band's front man, Ben Schneider, Sharon Emery's son. We have stayed in touch ever since, and over the years I've seen Lord Huron play several times. Whether on stage or one-on-one, there is an authentic gentleness and honest vulnerability to Ben, and I'm grateful for his music, and his friendship.

In January 2020, eight years after meeting Ben, I was fully progressed with ALS, living with the help of an incredible support system and adaptive equipment. But I was also busy establishing the Team Gleason foundation, which develops and provides technology to help ALS patients live better and longer. I am forever grateful that Congress voted to award me the Congressional Gold Medal, its highest civilian honor, for that work.

There were lots of details to be considered for the medal presentation, but when the organizers told me that I could have one musician perform one song, my choice was easy: Ben Schneider singing "Ends of the Earth." In the Capitol's historic Statuary Hall, filled with hundreds of guests, legislators, leaders of the House and Senate, media, family, and friends, Ben stepped up with his guitar and played.

Oh, there's an island where all things are silent,
I'm gonna whistle a tune.
Oh, there's a desert that size can't be measured,
I'm gonna count all the dunes.

My family and I will never forget that day at the U.S. Capitol. I said then that it was a "sublime honor" to be so recognized. But, more importantly, I hope the honor brought joy, encouragement, and even triumph, to the tens of thousands of extraordinary families living with ALS. I have that same wish for the millions of people living with disabilities and other illnesses, and more broadly, for all human beings experiencing adversity, tragedy, or anguish.

We did not know on that joyous day that just five weeks later COVID would challenge us all with adversities of epic proportion, for months and years to come. Ironically, having lived with ALS for a decade at that point, our family was prepared for that crisis on many levels. I have adopted the perspective that the trials that life brings us are opportunities. If we can grow to move through those trials, become more whole, and embrace the toughness of life, we can become more free.

In *It's Hard Being You*, Sharon Emery shares that same perspective in recounting her own experience with adversity, as well as that of her family. As the world shifts and evolves, human struggles are ever present. Although this book is a deeply personal journey, it's a timely and timeless lesson in acceptance as a pathway to our own peace.

Emery takes us intimately, sometimes painfully, through what it's like living with a disability and caring for someone with a disability. There are life lessons woven throughout the book, but Emery's message is clear that life isn't meant to be easy – for anyone. No one is immune from anguish, tragedy, or adversity. This is Sharon Emery's story, but it's also the human story.

Having stuttered severely all her life, Emery recognized the inequities her daughter, Jessica, who had cognitive impairments, was facing. As someone who can no longer move or speak or breathe on my own, I know something about this. Emery urges readers to be present in the experience of interacting with people with disabilities, who may not do things the way they do. And she admonishes them against imposing their able-bodied perspectives on people who are simply living with the body they were given. On a planet with almost eight billion people, it's time we embrace our differences.

There is power in Emery's telling of her story, including the heartbreak of her greatest loss – the death of her daughter Jessica, who lives on in these pages and in the lives of her family. This story provides healing, understanding, and empathy for others living with disability or caring for someone with a disability. It may even help them accept their struggle as a path to peace.

I met Ben through music and, specifically, a song about life as an adventure. It's not surprising that his mother would share her life experiences to assist others on their own journeys.

What good is livin' a life you've been given
If all you do is stand in one place.

Steve Gleason

November 2021

We tell ourselves stories in order to live.
—Joan Didion, *The White Album*

The Lodestar

To tell you where I'm coming from—and maybe who I really am—I have to set off a little bomb:

I am the mother of a dead child.

Forgive the brutality of that, but there is no word in the English language for this condition. Children who survive dead parents are orphans. But what are parents of dead children?

The death of my eldest child, Jessica, is not the center of my life. Yet it is undeniably the lodestar that has helped me align the crucial losses and limits I've faced and assign them meaning and purpose. This, I now know, is the overriding task of survival.

As life-ordering experiences go, few are as shattering as the death of a child. You need a tight hold on the essentials of existence to know how to bury your child. And how to survive it.

Miraculously, I've survived.

Saying flat out that my daughter died is explosive because death that close tends to startle people. They tense up, they look away, they struggle to find a word, any word that can stand up to the verbal assault of that news. "Sorry, I'm so sorry."

Sometimes they take a step back from me, as if to create distance between my tragedy and theirs. But here's the thing: Everybody knows the pain of loss and the struggle of limits, and everyone experiences them in their own way.

At first you are too stunned to do anything with "the tragedy," whichever one you're hit with. Not that it matters. They all come down to loss. And there is no comparing losses because your pain is yours alone. The reality of that has seared me, as you'll see. We are all suffering in some way, and we all have to figure out how to survive. It's not easy.

When my four children were little, struggling with the not-small issues children face (mean friends, scary tests), I would say, "It's hard being you." And while that statement sometimes took on a bit of snark when whining was involved ("My friends don't have to be home so early. . . ." "No one else has to do chores. . . ."), in general it was empathy. Life *is* hard.

Of course, those early losses and limits were just the beginning. My youngest, Caitlin, was fifteen years old when Jess died, and she asked me: "Is this the worst thing that will ever happen to me? Is this the last bad thing?"

The possible answers ricocheted in my brain as I

tried to determine the best one, the right one. I wanted to soothe her and say, "Yes, the worst is over. The rest of your life may be tough, but not this tough."

But another part of me didn't want to accept that my child had to endure such a crushing loss at all.

Ultimately, I recoiled at the thought of denying her pain, which brought me to what I think was the right answer: "You definitely will be happy again—I imagine very happy—but a happy life is destined to include suffering and heartbreak. It just is."

There's simply no getting around the fact that we pay dearly for our deepest joy, intimacy with others. When someone you've risked loving dies, a part of you dies with them. That's the bargain you strike when you boldly choose to love.

But when the severance involves your child, the loss—the amputation, if you will—is not surgical in any way. When you lose a child, that child is ripped from you. There are thousands, perhaps millions, of frayed edges where the child was torn out.

Yet there are myriad other losses and limits, and they are inevitable, despite our frantic efforts to avoid them. You hear a lot about unlimited possibilities, yet our options *are* limited, by everything from genes to circumstance.

But here's the inscrutable part: To succeed you need to *embrace* the limits that confront you, including all the losses that make you who you are—the slop of overshooting, the brokenness of falling short, the desolation of despair.

Surviving losses and living with the limits thrown at you is so central to making it through life intact that I'm amazed families spend so little time addressing the inevitable encounters with pain that are essential to a life. Perhaps the same optimism that draws us to produce children also permits us to think they can somehow escape unscathed.

But that is a disservice to children. No one is ever spared.

The truth of that makes me want to extend comforting arms into my children's suffering. Not to pull them out, but to help them proceed with gratitude and hope.

Limits, the loss of things—conditions, people we love—don't so much define our lives as empower us to shape them. I want my children to have that power. Harnessing it comes down to seeing the value of the good and the bad in our lives and assigning proportion to each. One helps us see the other; the good and bad are inextricably linked.

As Jessica's mom, I learned about that linkage amid all the challenges and joys she brought us as a person—our person—with developmental, cognitive and neurological differences. Families of people with disabilities know this split-screen life well. Among all the scream-out-loud moments, there are important lessons to be learned—not only for us but for the larger world we are helping create.

The families of people with disabilities are so

important. All of us grow and recede in relation to those we know most intimately and they, in turn, reflect back to us what we are. I suppose that's why the members of families can both love and hate each other with such passion—we see ourselves in each other.

By sheer proximity over time, family members bear witness to one another's lives—the mundane and the major, the quotidian and extraordinary. And what we see provides us with meaning and agency to help change the world. What we experience is important.

When Jess drowned—twenty years later, the specifics still cut me—I struggled mightily to make sense of what had happened to me, to my family. I needed someplace to put The Hole, the excruciating burden of negative space—the grief. I wanted to keep it within eyeshot, but not so close as to risk falling in, consumed by grief. It was tricky. Dangerous, even.

Standing wide-eyed in the blaring light of personal catastrophe, I learned that losing a relationship—losing love—is the cruelest burden we bear. No wonder estrangement and death are our deepest fears.

The first challenge was mere survival. One breath at a time, one night that led to a full day that led to another night and yet another day. Day Two. Somehow we, The Grieving, were still here. I imagined that it would take some specific action to continue, but it didn't. Time just washed over and past me. I was no longer the actor but the acted upon.

The first 133 days after Jess's death were treacherous. I made myself cry on each one of them. Every morning. For more than four months.

Then I started to write. I imagined that by attaching words to my grief I could give it shape and volume and mass, and that by creating it in time and space I could make it transportable—make it gone.

Where, I'm not sure.

Away, definitely, I wanted it away.

But strangely I also wanted it here forever. I wanted a record of my struggle with it. Like Jacob who wrestled with God and forever limped. I wanted my children to know that I endured grief at its most devastating. It diminished me to just a heartbeat and a whisper of breath on some days. On others I tried to defy it, angrily beating my fists against ... what? Fate? Happenstance? I was doing an amazing job being Jessica's mom, so why was that work taken away from me?

Ultimately, I realized my grief needed to declare itself: This happened, this tragedy happened *to me.* The telling was important because it allowed my isolated story to resonate as part of the shared human experience—bigger than me, bigger than you, bigger than everyone who stands to be consumed by grief.

After survival, learning how to proceed was my greatest challenge. I had to force myself to see beyond my grief, to the secrets emerging from my battle to survive. I had to break the secrets free from the struggle, so I could put them to work in my life.

I didn't want my grief to endure as tragedy, as a sad, unending story. And I definitely didn't want my children to see the loss of their sister, and their experience of that great loss, as tragedy. Tragedy requires an unhappy ending.

But Jessica's death was really just the beginning, the foundation for what I wanted to tell my children about learning to live with loss and limits. It's important because it's the key to a happy life.

Mining my own experience with loss and limits was grueling. And self-revealing. I initially tried to tell this story without acknowledging the lasting limitation of my own life: my stutter. I thought I was avoiding self-absorption, but, in fact, I was being less than brave.

I discovered that all my life I've feared being seen as "damaged," not quite right. So, I've defiantly cast myself as not only undamaged but the one who can walk through fire unscathed. It is much, much harder for me to say that I have regularly been burned. Hence my reluctance to acknowledge my battle with stuttering.

We all have to wrestle with our own limits, in a solitary battle we wage in our heads: How do I feel about this person who is me? We alone determine the impact of the events that comprise our lives.

Human beings have miraculous power to do this. We have survived for millions of years, not because we are smart or strong or even lucky, but because we are resilient. When bad things happen to us, we don't crumble, we adapt. We can even thrive. We have enormous capacity for happiness. In that, we truly *are* amazing.

What's extraordinary is when people don't survive. And there is some of that in this story. No denying, I'm the oldest of three siblings and the only one still here. My sister's and brother's stories showed me what a precarious balancing act it is to carry our experiences across the tightrope that is our life. Not everyone finds the equilibrium, the context that allows them to survive what happens to them.

Somehow, I did.

Essential truths can arise from the telling of our individual stories of adapting to loss and limits—the relentless but never mundane struggle to live as well as we can. This is mine.

Healing Dreams/Inner Voices

 One month after Jessica died—
Defending her life

I hurt for a long, long time—maybe forever—after life with Jessica in it ended.

I always knew I was hurting; I just didn't know I was also healing. Ever so slowly, I worked through my grief—in my dreams, and in my life. The melding of the two, dreams and life, was crucial, harrowing yet miraculous.

In both dreaming and living, grief advances and retreats, so it can surprise you, good and bad. The struggle is to give it meaning; it has to fit somewhere in your life story. Otherwise, grief is everywhere, and dangerous.

These healing dreams, and the waking-life insights that I call inner voices, unfold throughout this story and tell a tale all their own.

I had my first dream of Jessica. She had left for school but I didn't realize it, so I ran out of the house—left the door open (was that significant?)—and ran down the block to see her off.

She was in a station wagon, but it wasn't ours. It stopped in a driveway, and she walked back to me. I anxiously took her hand and asked how she was.

Jessica had on a purple-flowered T-shirt and she was very calm. She didn't grab me like she would have before. She just held my hand and said, "It was a lot of fun at the hearing."

But she was dissolving even as I tried to hold on to her. I woke up.

It was 7 a.m. of Day Twenty-Nine without her.

I thought the "hearing" was a reference to the Albert Brooks movie *Defending Your Life*. We watched that over and over during summers at our Lake Huron cottage. In the movie, when you die, your life is put up for review before a panel that decides if you have learned enough to move on, or if you have to return to Earth.

My dream was telling me that I just had to figure out where Jessica was.

And where I was.

Jessica Begins

As with all my pregnancies, carrying Jessica was no great burden. We got pregnant immediately—my husband, John, and I figured it was in Paris, when he was recovering from food poisoning (hamburger en route from Italy). But this was the City of Light ... and love! We were in Europe to celebrate our first anniversary and the American Bicentennial (smirk) which, as reporters at our small southwest Ohio newspapers, we were desperate to escape, having covered every conceivable local angle of that national celebration.

A few months after we returned from Europe, John got an offer to work for the *Lansing State Journal*. The lure of home, Michigan, was strong, the thought of our parents nearby and morphing into grandparents, a wonderful comfort.

I had been preparing to cover the inauguration

of Jimmy Carter as president in January 1977 for the *Troy* (OH) *Daily News*. (This was back when locally owned newspapers put resources into their product and literally brought national stories home to their readers.) Our moving plans put the kibosh on my chance to cover national politics. But three-months pregnant and nearing age twenty-five, I figured my future lay elsewhere.

We moved into a third-floor apartment on Abbot Road in East Lansing, not far from Michigan State University, where I planned to work on my doctorate—in my spare time, as a new mom. Yes, that's how delusional I was about the care and feeding of an infant. And how desperate I was to find my footing in a new place as a "trailing spouse," undefined by current employment and subject to anxiety concerning my nascent career.

The day before Jessica was born, we went to nearby Moon Lake to swim. My water broke that night, but there were no contractions, and I much preferred waiting at home. The next morning, while watching Jane Pauley (who was not much older than me) on the *Today* show, we decided it was time to go to Lansing's St. Lawrence Hospital.

It was packed on that summer day. There were so many women in labor that initially I was in a bed in the hallway. When I finally got into a semi-private room, John opened the bologna sandwich he had bought from a vending machine to fortify himself for the long haul. To this day the smell of bologna brings all of that back. I wanted to smack him; he took his dinner elsewhere.

A nurse came in to ask me the usual questions (when did my water break and when did contractions start?) and then added one specifically for me: Did I always talk this way (disfluently) or was it because I was in labor?

Ugg. Stuttering Education 101 had begun—again. The nurse's timing was bad, but—OK. "Yes, I always talk this way."

What I was thinking was, "No, I'm not so terrified of giving birth that I can't talk. I took Lamaze, for Pete's sake. So, yes, you have to get information from me in slo-mo, which I know is inconvenient and annoying—especially for me."

As is often the case with firstborns, the labor was laborious. There were some twenty-one hours from when my water broke until Jessica's birth, and I was determined to do it all without medication. By the time I cried uncle and asked for painkillers, they said it was too late—the baby would be born soon.

There were lots of student doctors in the delivery room, observing. Jessica was face up, or occiput posterior, so that's why it was taking so long. She couldn't get out. The doctor had to turn her with forceps to deliver her.

Many years later, when my RN friend first proposed it, I wondered about that process and whether the long labor may have cut off her oxygen and hurt her brain. We thought she had scored ten (the highest) on the APGAR, which measures the physical condition of newborns. Later, however, we learned her first score was much lower.

As a participating member of Motherhood, wherein we all grapple with whether our shortcomings are magnified in our offspring, I wondered if I had unwittingly done something during the pregnancy to cause her developmental delays: it was my fault.

But that was later. For about fifteen months we thought Jessica was the most perfect creature in the world.

Love has startling clarity at this point. My first-time-mother eyes couldn't take in all of the wonder of this person, this new life. I was amazed at having produced her and chose a name that reflected all my soaring hopes for her life: Jessica, which means "she who is wealthy in spirit." What could be better than having an abundant spirit to see my girl through whatever life would bring her?

Of course, I had no idea just how much spirit she would need.

Ultimately, we both spent a week in the hospital. Me, recovering from a bladder infection, and Jessica, my orange-tinged baby under lights in the hospital nursery, fighting off bilirubin as her liver adjusted to life in the world.

The homecoming to our East Lansing apartment was glorious: the nursery with the yellow theme (this was before routine tests for gender, so I chose my favorite color), the crib from my parents, newly minted Grandma and Grandpa Emery, and the Mary Cassatt print, "Mother and Child."

I was still recovering from the infection when John was out reporting one night on an East Lansing City Council meeting. I was shaking so severely that I was afraid to pick up Jessica. This is the most terrifying part of parenthood: to be right there and yet unable to help your child. (No matter their age. In fact, it only intensifies as children grow older and their steps more far-ranging.) I stayed by her crib and comforted her until John came home.

John and I soon conquered the basics of caring for our firstborn. And once we had that foundation laid, I started in on the task of memorializing the unique life Jessica was living, chronicling what I knew would be my daughter's amazing life.

Enter the scrapbook, conveyor and preserver of crucial details of even the smallest lives. Collecting and honoring those details is what mothers do. And I did it with a passion. I packed that scrapbook with everything relevant to the world's newest member: greeting cards sent to welcome her, the hospital receipt from her birth, and the pink plastic bracelet: Schneider, girl. 7:36 p.m., June 27, 1977.

I kept this up for several years, as the missives from admiring relatives marked her birthdays and holiday celebrations, and her early school artwork required post-refrigerator preservation.

But it wasn't long before those early scrapbook entries were replaced by the hostile takeover of school reports and medical files. Reams of paper and an ever-growing deluge of block-letter acronyms—POHI (physically or otherwise health impaired), LD (learning disabled), DD (developmentally delayed), ADHD (attention-deficit hyperactive-disorder), MI (mentally impaired)—that threatened to obscure Jessica's real identity as one of the world's wonders.

Increasingly, some saw her as impaired; we saw her as important, very important.

Ironically, I pasted in the final and most treasured scrapbook entry after Jess died: Mark Strand's poem "For Jessica, My Daughter" (from *Collected Poems*, Knopf, 2014). It was as if it had been written for *my* Jessica.

The poet expresses his anxious wish—indeed, the universal parental wish—to protect his child until the end of time, through the great darkness, into the vast unknown. Anticipating a time when he no longer would be there to guide her, the poet seeks to give his daughter something she can take with her, to find her way. He mentions a light, "a secret moon or mirror, a sheet of paper ... "

I liked that plan.

Each passing year brought more definition to Jessica's challenges. When at twelve months she wasn't walking, we signed her up for physical therapy. By fifteen months, she could walk. Problem solved.

At two-and-a-half, when she still wasn't

potty-trained, the local nursery school said she couldn't attend. But she qualified for special education services at a local public school based on her previous needs in learning to walk, so she got into a preschool and learned to use the toilet.

This also brought the first of the ever-encroaching labels, however. The teachers told us POHI (physically or otherwise health impaired) wasn't so bad, but that we should resist other labels (specifically, LD, learning disabled) that might put our daughter on a different, less desirable track. It was never clear exactly where that other track might lead, but we definitely wanted to avoid it.

Jess prospered at Lansing's North School and soon was within a few months of her expected development. Again, problem solved.

Kindergarten at our neighborhood Lansing school didn't work out (Jess would not sit still), so for first grade, we transferred her to the school one neighborhood over. This was a full-blown disaster. The school staff didn't know what to make of her "primitive" behavior (her first-grade teacher had referred to Jessica as a "monster"). Today I think they'd call it autistic. At the time it was sensory integration disorder. And who knew what else?

Then we moved to neighboring Okemos, where Jessica struggled at the local elementary school. Administrators there suggested a special program at another school in the district, led by a principal focused on helping children with special needs. The staff there encouraged us to push for further testing, which the district had been resisting, likely for money reasons. Eventually we succeeded, but the results were disheartening: likely cognitive impairment and some physical limitations.

Ultimately, the teachers suggested a special program in neighboring Haslett, where Jess seemed to thrive. For middle school and high school, it was back to Okemos, where they didn't seem to be as focused as we were on including special education students in regular classrooms.

I became known as the Mother from Hell, I'm sure. IEP (Individualized Education Program) meetings with staff were painful. It was the 1990s, and the school staff seemed to think we were shooting for the moon. I don't believe we ever convinced them of the advantages of inclusion—that non-disabled students could actually benefit from learning with disabled students like our daughter, and vice versa.

Miraculously, Jessica loved school, mainly because it was her primary social experience outside of our family. Many of the staff and teachers embraced her. School offered so many opportunities to talk, which she loved to do, and to just *be* with people—even people who didn't necessarily want to be with her.

A social worker at the high school helped us form a Circle of Friends group, students who volunteered to socialize with Jess outside of class. Friendship is a monumental challenge for people with disabilities, especially in high school, where it is tantalizingly on display but torturously out of reach.

For the first outing, the group was going to the mall. Jess was ready early, lipstick applied (a bit beyond her lips, which I tried to fix), waiting on our front porch.

She had bitten it all off by the time we realized they weren't coming. Apparently, there was a mix-up about the timing. I had to tell a tearful Jess it was hard being her.

Then we went to the mall to get her nails done. She proudly showed them off for the next two weeks.

Healing Dreams/Inner Voices

 Three months—Locking the doors

I had my second dream of Jessica, although she wasn't actually in the dream.

I dreamed I was in a room, and it was my job to lock out someone who was trying to get in. It wasn't easy because there were a lot of doors and many shiny, silver locks.

The would-be intruder wasn't scary, really, but I definitely didn't want him to get in.

Two women came through the building, on a tour or something. I made it seem like my job was no big deal as they passed through.

Containing Life

I've sketched the basic outline of who Jessica was, but fleshing out that portrait requires a glimpse into the everyday life of our family.

Tupperware is a good place to start. It was always missing.

Not just the lids (everyone has that problem), but lids *and* bowls—neat sets. Everything from the half-gallon bowl with the salad-spinner option to the shot-glass-size container that in a pinch could serve as an eye-washer.

And that was just the start of it. Once the Tupperware went missing, I knew the kitchen drawer that held the Ziploc bags would also have been plundered. The box that once held the two-quart bags, empty, and next to it, the rectangle of empty space where only recently I had put a one-hundred-count box of sandwich bags.

Technically, the bags and containers were not missing. I knew where they were. They were merely gone from where they had served me and put into service by Jessica, who used them to create a sense of order and control that most of us take for granted.

Jessica's developmentally disabled label got at many of her challenges, but not all. One doctor, I forget which one, described her problems simply as "global." That seemed to fit, as her challenges pretty much entailed her whole world. And ours.

The torment is that sometimes we parents don't live in the same world as our children. Instead, they inhabit parallel universes, and what lies between us is heartbreak.

I covet the experience of parents whose children wake up from bad dreams. Helping children cope with those dreams is one of the few pure victories of parenthood. Responding to a frantic scream in the night, your mere presence becomes a balm.

But there's more: you can totally envelope your child—in your arms and in your omniscience. You can explain away every fear, right down to the furry shadow projected on the wall by a stuffed animal propped too close to the nightlight. And soon just the sound of your voice is enough to bring sleep, and peace, to your child.

Trying to reach Jessica with that kind of reassurance was often impossible. We would beat on the wall that separated her experience from ours, but we couldn't get through. So, we were left to watch her screaming and writhing in that distant place.

As best we could understand, there were times when Jessica's experience of the world became a wild onslaught of sight, sound and touch. The catalyst was usually something unexpected, or something much-anticipated. That's just how unpredictable the onset was.

Her experience was so intensely painful that she would lash out at everything, often at what she loved best. She smashed her Walkman, she hit her friend, she put her foot through a double-pane window. (It was safety glass, so she wasn't hurt. At least, there was no blood.)

But she did suffer the loss of her precious music, and a companion who no longer came to the phone when she called. As for the four-by-six-feet window wall, my husband and I popped the tabs on two cans of beer and just sat, staring at the carnage.

Jessica was on the floor nearby, wailing in regret. "Do you take the apology?" she pleaded.

"Uh, huh," we nodded, dazed, like the survivors of a tornado trying to get a fix on the loss.

On the countless times I went to Jessica's bedroom (bedecked in purple, her favorite color) to retrieve the Tupperware and plastic bags, she was always glad to see me. Even though she knew I had come to dismantle her Shangri-La.

She would be on her bed, surrounded by all the opulence plastic could contain: her hairbrush in

Tupperware, her videotapes in Ziploc, her rings in a little cup. The containers and bags covered every available surface of her night table, her dresser, her entertainment center. Her world was spread before her, and for those precious moments it had an order of her own devising.

I never took back everything on those rescue missions. I would find out which containers held the most comfort for her and let her keep those. One time it was the four-by-four-inch Tupperware container with the *Charlotte's Web* tape in it, and a plastic bag caging a lavender stuffed animal.

I could live with that. Without what remained, I assumed she could not.

Eventually I came to understand the importance of such objects. They were the armor Jessica needed to get through the sensory barrage of being in the world. Who knew what comfort she derived from painstakingly recording names and addresses in her notebooks, or why she hoarded pens and pencils and always asked for more for her birthday? We just knew that she needed them.

There were people in Jessica's room, too. People in photos who never moved, never changed. Sometimes they would appear in duplicate, thanks to two-for-one specials at the photo shop. While the duplicates were meant to give away, Jessica displayed them as identical pairs. The formal poses were framed. But most were tiny Polaroid snapshots of the most important things in her world: her teachers and classmates, her dad and me, her siblings, Harry Potter, and her dear, departed cat Tiffany.

She surrounded herself with these immutable images, carrying as many of them with her wherever she went, so that when the real world came roaring in, she could take refuge in the comforting familiarity of their faces. A frightening blur of people might be passing as she walked through the mall, but as long as she could focus on the smiling face of Keith Froelich, the high school football coach (indulgently posing with his secretary in the athletic office), she could make her way through the onslaught.

Her room also featured a bulletin board devoted to Michigan Governor John Engler (who served 1991-2003), a man not known for his physical beauty, or even his charm. Two framed photos on the other side of her entertainment console balanced out the bulletin board. In one, Jessica had just met the governor after a press conference. She had him in a kind of loving headlock, which she agreed to pull back on a bit for the photo. The governor was smiling bravely.

Michelle Engler and their triplet daughters were featured in the other photo, which was signed with a personal greeting. Having sent regular Christmas cards to the Englers, Jessica had made her presence known in the upper echelons of state government—thanks to Sarah, a family friend who knew the governor well enough to ask a favor.

Why the governor? He was an icebreaker.

Want to get somebody's attention? Tell them you've

Jess and former Michigan Governor John Engler, at a news conference for the release of her dad's book about Richard Prangley, who was wrongly institutionalized by the state. (1998) Photo by Paul Tarr.

met the governor. Want to make an impression? Tell them you're the proud owner of the governor's official Christmas ornament, which featured three Snowbabies with the initials of the Engler triplets hand painted on their scarves. Besides the weather and sports, there's nothing like name dropping to get even people who are resisting to engage you.

And they did resist. There was something off-putting, after all, about a grown woman—or at least she looked grown—who insisted on making a physical connection with you. She had learned that her words were too easy to ignore, people did it all the time. So, Jessica devised a system that guaranteed a response: it required them to pose a question that only she could answer.

"Ask me how I feel," she'd say.

At first her conversation targets didn't understand that it was a setup, so they just obligingly posed the question.

"I feel GREAT!" she'd respond, moving on to the next tactic to maintain her listener's interest. She'd grab both of their arms just above the elbow and give them a little shake. "Can you BELIEVE it?" As if the status of her health were the most anticipated news of the day.

"Wanna get happy?" she'd continue. Now, really, who could resist that offer? "Michigan State beat Minnesota!" she'd say, as if her joy should be theirs. And she did want it to be; she was giving it to them.

It didn't much matter if they recoiled. It happened

often enough that she was willing to indulge people for a while, give them an opportunity to meet the occasion. Then, if they embraced her, they were engaged in a moment so real it hurt. They were with her, whether they wanted to be or not.

Early on, my questions about Jessica's challenges were fundamental: How did this happen? And why? You prepare for pregnancy, you eat a balanced diet, you see your doctor, you forgo drugs during childbirth, you breast feed.

And yet, something goes wrong, in a slow unraveling of every fear that has ever haunted any parent. Suddenly, those fears are all yours. The "how" of it is so inexplicable that you don't even want to go for the "why."

The lucky thing is that the whole of Jessica was not deficits. But the truth of that came as a slowly evolving revelation. "Disabled" was her primary identity in the world, the persistent adjective used to describe her various roles: the disabled student, the disabled worker, that disabled woman over there . . .

True, Jessica didn't think like your typical twenty-something. She was never able to read much beyond a first-grade level, and counting more than three objects made her so frustrated that she was liable to deck the nearest person as she struggled with the task. Her siblings developed split-second timing in knowing when to duck, keeping an internal scorecard in the Olympian experience of growing up with Jessica.

Yet when we got lost while exploring a new city on family vacations, she was the one who could get us back to our hotel, having tracked landmarks in a way that my husband and I simply did not. She had developed some compensatory skills and may even have fostered abilities others didn't have. Ken, the school bus driver, told us Jessica was the only student on his bus who ever wished him a happy Thanksgiving.

As a first-born, Jessica was always the given in the sibling scenario. Her brothers and sister had to do the adjusting, as all younger siblings do. Adding substantially to their task, however, was their sister's disability, and I fretted long and hard about what that would mean for how they viewed themselves and the world.

How bad was it when Jessica threw a fit on the school bus because someone sat in her special seat and her younger sister had to slink to the back to escape the hot, loud laughter of the other kids? How painful was it when the sound of the school band caused Jessica to launch into a verbal tirade, with members of the pep-assembly crowd knowingly pointing fingers at her brother? "That's Justin's sister."

If only life with Jess had been a half-hour sit-com, or even a two-hour movie, we could have presumed that all those coming into contact with her would be profoundly and magnificently changed.

As we were.

Healing Dreams/Inner Voices

 Five months—Bodies at her wake

I had a dream that I think is connected to the last one, about the locked doors.

We were having a wake or memorial service for Jessica at our house, and lots of people were invited.

Just before the guests arrived, I realized that we had some dead, bloody bodies in the house. Strangely, that wasn't shocking to me; I had heard such things were happening in the area. My father was one of the bodies, but since I knew he was already dead, I didn't panic. My main concern was that the bodies didn't disrupt the event.

In both this dream and the last one I was trying to ensure that life went on as planned. But the job seemed easier when it just involved locked doors, not dead bodies.

Stuttering Me

Having a disability myself made me hyper-aware of the need to beat down social constructs—the larger world's opinion of what you can and cannot do—that prevent people with disabilities from reaching their full potential. Over time you get angry enough, and then brave enough, to be ferocious in that mission.

Society creates a host of barriers around not just disability, but skin color, gender, physical size, sexual orientation, age, socioeconomic status, you name it.

That means we all have to determine which of the valuable-but-hard-to-appreciate limits and losses we face are real, and which are constructs—of others' expectations, of our own expectations, of our demons.

As a young woman I resisted acknowledging that any of my limits and losses—especially stuttering—were real, as in permanent. They were just there until I overcame them. If I didn't, I was failing.

I guess that's how Driven became my middle name.

Eventually I came to realize that there are some things you simply cannot change. Those are the losses and limits that are real—and that's not necessarily a bad thing, as you'll see. It turns out that once you determine which losses and limits are real, you have the power to find a place for them in your imperfect but glorious, unfolding life.

In my case, I could be a stuttering journalist, rather than the fluent reporter I was trying to be. That was the reality of the situation in a field that emphasizes verbal communication and fluency. I just had to convince the people in charge that I could do it.

Newsrooms in the 1970s and 1980s didn't necessarily champion diversity in their ranks, and even if they had, I doubt stuttering would have been mentioned. Even today it's not, and diversity is all the rage.

As recently as 2020, a study by Elia Powers ("The Journalist's Speech: A Phenomenological Study of Stuttering in the Newsroom") found that, "Stuttering did not dissuade most participants from pursuing and sustaining a news media career, but it commonly limited career options and led colleagues to question their competency before they had proven themselves professionally."

So, yeah, you have to face the possible immutability of your situation, but then you have to buckle down for the really hard work: you have to start battling the limits that are constructs—what society thinks you can and cannot do. If you think tackling your inner demons is tough, you have to be even braver in knocking down society's hurdles as you run your leg of the race in making an equitable world. This is a lifelong endeavor.

I often had the nagging sense throughout my career that while my employers had obviously been willing to give me a chance, they were prepared to see it end badly. But maybe that was the story as seen by a fearful person—me. Maybe my employers were expecting me to succeed, and I was terrified of failing them.

After almost two years at my first reporting gig at the *Troy Daily News*, we moved to Lansing for John's job. Six months later I became Jessica's mom, and three months after that I started a doctorate at Michigan State University in mass media, which was actually a thing in the 1970s. While I ultimately abandoned my course of study (a bustling newsroom proved more enticing than academia), I continued to teach journalism at MSU on a part-time basis for the next ten years as my four children were being born.

When my youngest was eighteen months old, I went back to full-time work at the Lansing Bureau of what was then Booth Newspapers, now Mlive. As assistant news editor, with day-to-day oversight of the Lansing, Detroit and Washington bureaus, I kept my credo posted at eye level at my desk: Hold everything to strictest scrutiny. And I did; this was perhaps my most important work.

During my twenty years at Booth, I made close ties

with coworkers who became lifelong friends. We were a family in the sense of encouraging each other to do our best work and supporting each other when things went haywire in our professional or personal lives.

When the newspaper industry started imploding in the mid-aughts and I needed to reinvent my working self, I became vice president at Truscott Rossman, a Lansing-based strategic communications/public relations firm. One of the owners of the company, Kelly Rossman-McKinney, confided that a client assigned to me questioned if I was the best fit for them, citing my stutter.

"I can give you someone else, but if you want the best, Sharon's the best," she told her. And I *was* the best. I made sure of it. (The client stayed with me.)

Diminished expectations hurt not only the person being underestimated but also the person/employer doing the underestimating—they miss out on what an empowered employee can do.

Since I had some history in battling social constructs in my own life, I was more than ready to help Jessica, too. So, to give you the full picture of where I was coming from as Jessica's mom, here's the backstory of how I got to be me.

I was the miracle baby born to John and Oliefa Emery, nearly ten years after they married in 1943, and not long after they had decided to adopt after years of trying to conceive. My mother's late-in-life pregnancy (at thirty-five!) was seen as requiring special attention, and the nuns at St. Joseph Hospital in Mount Clemens, Michigan, were there to provide it (even though we weren't Catholic).

I was wonderful, my parents assured me, hence my abiding aspiration to give the world a big ... *something*. Every day I went to school, and later work, with that purpose in mind. I had to let the world know that I was indeed wonderful, despite my disfluency, which seemed to signal dysfunction in a world that embraced the garrulous.

As a result of my lofty aspirations, I accomplished more than I might have—Ivy League grad school, prestigious journalism fellowship, solid career. But truth be told, for most of my life I wondered why no one had "discovered" me. I mean, I was brilliant, engaging, talented and all-around wonderful. World, wake up!

I knew I had to speak up. But how, with this staccato voice?

My voice was first brought to my attention in second grade, when my teacher suggested I see the school speech therapist. My parents later told me they hadn't been particularly concerned about it, but they had every faith in public education and thought it was worth a try. Over the next decade, I worked with several therapists who used a variety of techniques, but my stutter proved recalcitrant.

I, however, certainly wasn't. I practiced every technique suggested and continually (as much as I could bear) put myself into speaking situations. So as to gain confidence, my instructors said. Of course, when there's no success—standing before an expectant audience, mute except for the extended first sound of a first word that never comes—you have to persist like hell just to make sure the world doesn't forget you're there. Even in all your brokenness.

I have marveled that bullied, ridiculed Joe Biden, as described by John Hendrickson in his interview with Biden for *The Atlantic*, just pushed through to overcome stuttering. For some reason I had failed to overcome, despite all my pushing.

But the fear of speaking, the shame of being "less than," the threat of being labeled mentally inferior all seem to have made Biden—and me—sensitive to criticism and prone to embellishment, to make up for our shortfalls.

Luckily, I was shocked—defibrillated, if you will, in a most profound way—into realizing the dangers of exaggerating my accomplishments when in fifth grade I told a friend that I had been promoted, and her parents overheard. They were impressed and asked what that would mean for me.

I was stunned, of course. What now?!

From somewhere within my frantically swimming brain, I grabbed hold of this: my mother had told me that when she was in school, there were A and B contingents to her class. OK, that might work.

I began struggling physically (with my stutter)

and emotionally (I had been caught in a whopper!) to explain that I had simply gone from 5B to 5A.

And then I got out of there, never again to dabble in exaggeration or anything close. I knew that I had to start racking up certifiable achievements in numbers beyond the ordinary.

During grade school and through high school I had my share of taunting and bullying to put up with. Mostly kids mimicking my blocked speech or avoiding talking to me because the experience was so weird. Still, I was a fairly popular kid. Not the prom queen, but close to her circle and sometimes even on her court (ninth grade).

I attribute this to two things: I had a good sense of humor (from my mother), making me as personable as a stuttering person could be. And I was a good-looking kid, which often got me in the door when I could be disciplined enough to keep my mouth shut.

There was a time when keeping my mouth shut seemed the only way to go. As a teenager I enlisted Jan, my younger sister by three years, to initiate phone calls to my friends, so as to avoid my friends' parents hanging up as I choked in silence on the other end.

And it was terrifying to sit in class, waiting with dread for my turn to read a textbook passage. I found out I could actually make myself sick anticipating that humiliation, which allowed me to avoid it for a while. At that point being sick was preferable to being disfluent.

In my teens, I was haunted by the realization that

my speech could be detrimental to the growing list of things I wanted to do, such as become a journalist. (That ambition took hold in sixth grade, when I edited my elementary school newspaper, the *Wellington Gazette*.)

As high school graduation approached, my identity crisis hit—specifically my determination to defy being labeled a stutterer. Well-meaning counselors were assuming that identity for me in recommending career options: teaching preschool, where the kids wouldn't mind my stutter (before the era of helicopter parents) or being an auto show model (before they actually had to talk).

My speech pathologist, on the other hand, thought I should be a lawyer. I knew I needed to stick around people like him.

At my request, the high school speech therapist referred me to specialists within Michigan, and I made graduation my final deadline for getting fluent.

When that didn't take, I vowed to be my own therapist while in college, applying with desperate intention all the techniques I had learned. I loved college, and even slogged my way through French dictation. But I still stuttered.

College also introduced me to Samuel Johnson's *The History of Rasselas, Prince of Abissinia*, where in chapter six the mechanist tells the philosopher that all creatures have their own element for accomplishing their purpose:

". . . fishes have the water, in which yet beasts can

swim by nature and man by art. He that can swim needs not despair to fly; to swim is to fly in a grosser fluid, and to fly is to swim in a subtler. *We are only to proportion our power of resistance to the different density of matter through which we are to pass.*"

That was it: I needed to buck up! I just had to summon my powers to take me where I wanted to go. A recurrent entry in my journal conveyed the grueling nature of this task: The key is to just keep swimming.

I went to Wayne State University in Detroit, declaring a double major in English (so I'd have the background to write well) and journalism (so I could support myself.) Above all, I knew I had to be better—a lot better—than my fluent peers.

I was named one of two Most Outstanding Journalism Graduates in the Spring 1974 class and worked three part-time journalism jobs during my senior year. I was news editor at the WSU student newspaper, *The South End*; classified ad editor at the *Detroit Free Press* (where I met John, who was a copy boy); and stringer at the *Community News* in Macomb County.

Still, I worried that wasn't enough to make me employable. I looked good on paper, but when I opened my mouth—damn. I figured I had to shoot for the leading journalism school in the country, the Graduate School of Journalism at Columbia University in New York City. It was the only school

I thought could help lift me above my stutter in the eyes of employers.

Meanwhile, I was corresponding with a newspaper in Pompano Beach, Florida, about a feature writing job. I struggled for fluency throughout the phone interview, which I feared would kill my chances, even though they had been impressed with my Women in Communications Scholarship.

But before they could reject me, I was accepted at Columbia. Hallelujah!

My parents—who had never visited New York City and never particularly wanted to—drove me there over the Labor Day weekend, 1974. The first part of the journey included John following us in his red Plymouth Satellite, as he drove back to Sidney, Ohio, where he was living. Long before cell phones, I remember writing last-minute messages and holding them up in the back window for him to read.

My savvy roommate had arrived first and commandeered the prized back room of our two-room suite, so my parents helped me move into the first room at 804 Johnson (now Wien) Hall, on 116th Street between Amsterdam Avenue and Morningside Drive.

Then they left, no doubt with some trepidation about how Sis (my dad's nickname for me) was going to make it in the Big Apple.

No worries. Attending Columbia in the mid-1970s was thrilling. It was after the explosive student protests of the 1960s, but I imagined a charge in the air that made me think something exciting could still happen at any time. Gentrification hadn't yet taken hold on the Upper West Side and Morningside Park was not safe. Still, it was New York City! And I was there to live, work, explore and study.

I was enthralled by legendary TV newsman Fred Friendly's lectures, his stories and convictions, and inspired by many of my classmates. They were smart and talented, but no more so than me. It was an important lesson.

I knew I could be a terrific journalist; I just had to keep convincing other people. I had to overcome their low expectations.

Exhibit A, in an evaluation from one of my instructors at Columbia:

> "*A bright and committed student, Miss Emery has done good work. She has evident capacity and she should work on her stutter, which could be a handicap in conducting interviews.*"

And this was an editing class, where interviews weren't even an issue.

As if I hadn't been trying my whole life to work on my stutter! (Plus, it wasn't *my* stutter, it was just the stutter I had to deal with.)

And worse, as if my "evident capacity" was threatened by who I was, a person who stuttered. That is the excruciating pain of being a person with a disability—diminished expectations. I spent the year determined to overcome them.

I graduated from Columbia in May 1975, as the economic recession of 1973-1975 was ending. John and I married three weeks later in Detroit, hoping to start life together as two working journalists. We had decided earlier that year, while sitting in NYC's Washington Square on a beautiful spring day, that we would live wherever at least one of us had a job and the other could find one.

True to form, I shot for the moon—targeting the *New York Times* and *Newsday*—but didn't make the cut. So, I moved into John's flat in Sidney, Ohio, after we married and started beating the bushes for work.

I was lucky and talented enough to get a reporting job at the *Troy Daily News*, just twenty miles down the road. On my first day, the editor told me straight out that he wouldn't avoid throwing me stories because of my stutter. I was in heaven.

But I still stuttered. And I didn't want to.

In my mid-twenties, I did two tours of stuttering therapy at the Hollins Communications Research Institute in Virginia, which I was sure would lead to fluency. An instructor there was a long-time stutterer and now didn't stutter!

But that didn't turn out to be the cure, either.

Then when I was as a doctoral candidate and part-time instructor at MSU, I found a therapist there and worked with him on and off for about twenty years, even trying relaxation therapy and hypnosis.

But I still stuttered.

Healing Dreams/Inner Voices

 Six months—Found: her book

A water pipe burst in our attic right above Jessica's bedroom and I was forced to go through her things, having quickly packed them away in her closet when she died.

I found her *Sweet Valley High* books about twins Elizabeth and Jessica, and my husband's *Kin* books, compilations of his newspaper columns about our family, inscribed just for her. And then a slim paperback *Missing May*. The back cover said it was about a young girl coming to grips with a death.

That night in bed I started reading.

Summer was a twelve-year-old girl who had lived with her loving aunt and uncle since she was six. It was February during a frigid winter not unlike the one we were having. Summer and her uncle were still trying to get over the death of her Aunt May in August—the same month Jess died. Summer's friend

Cletus was an odd but insightful boy who was fascinated with photos of people, which he carried around in a box just as Jessica did.

I knew beyond question that Jessica had sent me the book to let me know she was okay. I read it twice and was eager to let others know the miraculousness of it all.

But I got only bewildered nods.

Stuttering Me, cont.

J ust before Jessica was born in June 1977 and before starting the doctoral program at Michigan State University in September (another notch on my career belt—Dr. Emery!), I wrote the passage below in my journal.

Having just attended the stuttering fluency program at Hollins Communications Research Institute—a considerable investment, considering our family budget and my own desperation to succeed—the pressure was on to finally conquer stuttering.

There was also the dreaded realization that full-time reporting had proved to be a huge physical and emotional challenge. Every day, with every interview, I had to beat back the fear of failure. So far, I had succeeded, but when would I fail? And I hadn't expected the physical toll. What if I couldn't do my very best

because the struggle to speak was so exhausting?
The thought tortured me.

*Defining one's self—how requisite, but adoles-
cent. To be at it again. Limbo, again. Where are
all the guideposts I've laid down? There, but
yet to be posted. My job, again. To find the way,
again. Somewhere between Sidney, Ohio, and
East Lansing, with fleeting sojourns to New York,
Detroit. Me, in all of those places, now here. The
same me in all those places but not the same me.
So, to redefine myself, here, at a time when my
decisions are so crucial—between motherhood and
childlessness, returning to reporting or school, and
now (finally) possibly, between control of and continued subjection to that tyrant: stuttering. The one
aspect of my life that's trying to prove itself more
powerful than my will. A defeat I have not and will
not accept (though I've weakened at times). Because
there's no way my composition calls for that definition: stutterer. And I refuse to be commanded by
influences not of my own nature.*

*Sometimes I wonder how I can still believe—and
I do, at the very core of who I am—that I can free
myself of this verbal paralysis. After all the dead-
lines I've set: graduating from sixth grade, getting
my braces off, entering college, going to graduate school, getting married, starting a career. . .
And all the daily resolutions . . . prepared with*

such determination as I lie in bed each night. Determination reinforced by bad dreams of stumbling, waking with certainty of success: today ... is ... The ... Day. Then proceeding with utmost caution ... careful, carefully. Then (oh, no!) to hesitate. And stumble. And fall. Then, hurting, but continuing anyway. Not with any skill, but just to persevere.

I write myself instructions to be followed each and every day, each and every hour, each and every second. So as not to fail at fluency. And, yet, to fail. Each ... and every ... time.

Talk slowly and deliberately

Don't struggle—stutter easily

Stutter slowly

Talk in a firm voice

Use natural inflection

Don't repeat

Note fluent speech

Talk often

Resist time pressure

Eliminate secondary symptoms

Overcorrect blocked words: slow, sliding speech

Pause before feared word and relax

In block, slow down block and make a smooth
    prolongation of it

In a certain, very crucial way, I no longer feel in control. I've decided I can't bear being a reporter or even a teacher while remaining a stutterer.

And to my bitter dejection—and, to be honest, deepest shock—I haven't yet been able to throw off the stuttering.

But, of course, I could bear it; and I did—I just kept swimming, as Samuel Johnson had advised. "Overcoming" would have been the great achievement, but there was none of that. So, I just kept going, trying to get the world to see the wealth of contributions stored inside me, just waiting to be unleashed.

Alternately, I guess you could say I persisted in banging my head against the wall. "Believe in yourself and you will go far," Charles Payne, my fifth-grade teacher at Wellington Elementary, had written in my Girl Scout autograph book. Got it.

But believing in myself was an ongoing struggle. A few years after the journal entry above, before starting a new term teaching journalism at Michigan State, I wrote this in a reporter's notebook:

How do I feel about starting a new term? Terrified. Not so much at the prospect of facing new students and teaching them; I've done that and do it well.

Rather, terrified at the prospect of all the pain—physical and emotional—I know I'll have to undergo in the process.

I've plunged into these things without regard for my feelings—just for the achievement, the outward guise of "success." But that's a success you can never be comfortable with because it's never secure.

The foundations—the good feelings about and within your self—aren't there. And so, you keep building up these outward successes in an effort to get that security. Meanwhile denying that impeded speech is a problem. Committed, in fact, to proving it's not.

Taking on these challenges to create this person— this image—without taking into account the toll those challenges take on the person underneath the façade. Creating this outer person at the expense of my inside person. I could keep this up as long as I was seeing satisfactory results in my outside person—"success," honors, etc.

When, finally, my outside person wasn't doing well—in the PhD. program, for instance, when I was struggling to maintain a 3.0 GPA—I created other reasons for staying in the program I hated: setting a precedent for other women, especially women with children, in going back to school. I was the only woman in the program with a child, and I'd give all striving women a bad name if I quit. I wasn't staying just for me; I was being altruistic.

Since then, I've found that there's a difference between resisting limitations and building on them. In resisting, you're always pushing to get out from under something. In acknowledging, you stand apart from your limitations: "There they are, nothing to see here."

Then you start building on them, simply by acknowledging they exist. Your limits, paradoxically, become the foundation for your accomplishments, your contributions to the world.

But acknowledging limits, let alone using them as building blocks, isn't easy. For a long time, I tried desperately *not* to be a stutterer. Most everything I did was based on that. Ostensibly, I was doing things *despite* stuttering.

But I think I was really doing them *because* of it. I never wanted stuttering to control my life, but it very definitely had. Because I had this "problem" called stuttering, I pushed myself to prove that I didn't have a problem. So devoted was I to this project that I had to carry around a huge façade for a big part of my life.

Of course, there is an inner experience to that outward façade: denial of all the pain I've been through. So let me just say, I have been pained. (And I've also been a pain, as many—especially my children and certain reporters—know.)

The well-meaning, gentle prod, "Keep trying, one day you'll succeed," can bludgeon and terrorize. When you're "brave" every day, with every speaking breath you take, the intended inspiration of the "be strong" message becomes your dreaded mandate, your crucible.

There is wisdom in the internet meme: "Courage is knowing it might hurt and doing it anyway. Stupidity is the same. And that's why life is hard."

All famous stutterers—James Earl Jones, Emily Blunt, President Biden—are people who no longer stutter in an obvious way. Where's the inspiration in that? "Overcoming" is much celebrated—the battle fought and won, hail to the victors. "Enduring" and "persevering," much less so. Those soldiers are still battling—and bloody.

For nearly half my life, I battled to fight off stuttering. But it fought ferociously to stay with me. The fast-talking world doesn't tolerate the verbally enfeebled and often erroneously assumes that disfluency means stupid, or too weak to "overcome" stuttering. For a long time, I lived in fear of those labels and their ability to stifle my aspirations. Porky Pig was not a good role model. But at least he was just a stuttering pig.

Try finding a woman character who stutters in popular culture or fiction. While there are men who stutter—Bill Denborough (unofficial leader of the Losers Club) in Stephen King's *It,* Ken Pile in the infamous (to people who stutter) film *A Fish Called Wanda,* and young Simon (the future Duke of Hastings, whose father declared him an "idiot") in Netflix's *Bridgerton,* come to mind —there are essentially no women who stutter. The only one I know of—Merry Levov in Philip Roth's *American Pastoral*—has haunted me since she first appeared in the 1997 Pulitzer Prize-winning novel. Merry is an angry young woman who commits political terrorism and ends up murdering four people. She miraculously loses her stutter when working with her weapon of choice, dynamite. Her stutter is her defining characteristic.

What stuttering female wants that as a reference point? When there are so few portrayals of women who stutter in popular culture, misdrawn depictions fill the vacuum. I can only hope women stutterers—about one-quarter of the one percent of people who stutter—can forge their own identity. Of course, I've always assumed it starts with me.

Speech is tightly woven into identity. Just watch the political skits on *Saturday Night Live.* The comedians look somewhat like their characters, but it's the idiolects—the vocabulary, pronunciation and grammar of each unique individual—that make the skits so real.

While we all speak at the same rate online—and that has often been a blessing for me—there is value in the sound of your own voice, no matter its rating on the fluency meter.

In my early thirties, as part of my increasingly desperate search to prove I was not defective, I went to a psychotherapist to figure it out. Maybe my psyche was the problem and I just had to learn how to fix it.

Over several months, my therapist and I determined that my family life growing up was not perfect. My parents used alcohol to cope with their limits, and the unpredictability of when that would happen was distressing to me as a kid. My mother drank wine to cope with what I later understood to be episodes of depression that seemed to run in her family. And I

*Ralph, me and Jan with our parents
at their fiftieth wedding anniversary party. (1993)*

think my father drank bourbon to relieve stress when he worked long stretches of overtime at the shop, anxious about keeping his family out of the poverty he grew up in.

My parents were married fifty-two years until my father died, and I think they really loved each other. (Coupling is complicated.) There was no doubt they loved us kids, and once I became a parent myself, I looked back and decided that they had done the best they could. For all their mistakes, there was that.

On the other side of the ledger, the therapist helped me realize that I currently had: 1) a successful family life; 2) a successful professional life; 3) a successful social life; and 4) a successful community life.

Maybe my stutter wasn't such a bad thing.

What?! I had never considered that! My stutter wasn't my bad?

It was a shocking revelation.

Stunning, tumultuous, life-changing. (Remember, this was before the disability pride movement.) I was freed from the tyranny of trying to fix myself.

Ironically, with that perspective it became *more* difficult for me to acknowledge that stuttering has been a monumental challenge. I remained battered by those social constructs around disability that say if you're still struggling with it, you remain damaged— even though I could now blithely respond that, yeah, stuttering is just something I have to deal with.

Eventually I was brave enough to acknowledge that I've suffered as a stutterer in this fluency-based world, but I've put my own spin on it. My TEDx Talk from 2011 (more on that later) lays out the process involved: noting the pain, but then working toward a broader, more enlightened perspective.

In my case, that included considering exactly whose problem my stutter was. Note the title of my talk: "The Disabled Listener." That perspective—choosing a different interpretation of the experience of stuttering—allowed me to view my squirming listeners with compassion (and also a little snark) and suggest a better route for them and me. Suddenly I was in control.

Putting words to all this has been excruciating, but of course that's the way I roll. A persistent, prodding (fluent, even) voice kept telling me I had something to say that needed permanency. The problem is that eventually we run out of time, so it's best to get on with it. I've been lucky; time has been tapping its toe on me for quite a while. (I take some comfort in knowing that Grandma Moses was seventy-eight when she began painting in earnest.)

My Grandpa Diebel (my mother's father) died when I was ten, President Kennedy when I was eleven, my Girl Scout friend Sandy when I was thirteen, Martin Luther King Jr. and Bobby Kennedy the year I turned sixteen, various aunts, uncles and John Lennon in my twenties, my cousin Joyce when I was thirty, my church friend Kathy when I was forty, my father when I was forty-two, my mother when I was forty-six, my daughter and my sister when I was fifty, my brother when I was fifty-nine, my childhood friend Joyce when I was sixty-five.

The ticking sound was getting closer.

I've wrestled with the value of limits for much of my life. I think most writers are drawn to writing by their limitations—the need to articulate their experience so that others can bear witness and perhaps proceed with some new knowledge.

I am, of course, supremely disfluent. But, in fact, all of my vocal abilities are impaired. As a person who cannot carry a tune, I am also supremely disharmonious. (That's a shame because stutterers don't stutter when they sing.) I marvel at singers who can belt out a tune, my son Ben included.

I marvel when he takes the stage as Lord Huron, recounting life's sometimes solitary search in "Long Lost" (*"I've got a place in the world and I found out where: out in the night all alone in the Way Out There, I ain't lonely, I'm long lost*), or proclaiming the triumph of coming "Back from the Edge" (*"Where you go when you die, I fell back down to Earth, Through a hole in the sky, I crashed into the sea, Then somehow I survived"*). He succumbs to despair and regret in "The Night We Met" (*"I had all and then most of you, Some and now none of you, Take me back to the night we met"*) and even looks for Jessica "In the Wind" (*"I would wait for*

*Lord Huron headlined at the 10,000-seat Red Rocks
Ampitheatre, Morrison, Colorado. (2019)*

a thousand years, I would sit right here by the lake, my dear, You just let me know that you're coming home, And I'll wait for you"). What a catharsis that must be!

I once took lessons from an opera singer who was trying to earn extra money. I just wanted to be able to sing "Happy Birthday" to my husband.

I learned a lot, mostly about my limits. She told me that most people sing in the keys of E or F, but I sing in C major. Moreover, people have a singing voice and a speaking voice, the opera singer explained, but my singing voice was not in my body yet. (Which is the nicest thing anyone has ever said about my singing voice.)

After a few lessons, she suggested I might want to quit. I guess you could say I failed, but the trying made me feel better. Ditto for all the speech therapy I had over the years: I tried, I was still swimming. (Hat tip again to Samuel Johnson.)

No one could accuse me of not at least attempting to better myself. Looking back, I think I worked hard and worried hard, trying to prove that I wasn't wallowing in my inabilities—that I realized my staccato speaking voice and tuneless singing voice didn't make the grade.

But I *had* to keep speaking. Because *not* using my voice was even more painful than using it. It actually came down to that.

I would struggle to make a point in a room full of people—heart racing, lips trembling, mouth jammed in what could possibly be a never-ending block.

My audience was by turns uncomfortable, wishing it was over and, most disappointing of all, focused on my delivery instead of my words.

The horror of all that was somehow better than staying silent. I guess it all came back to that *something* I always knew was there, and I just *had* to get it out. I didn't want my contributions to the world to implode inside me.

So, I talk. (And even sometimes sing—once the coast is clear of unwitting listeners.)

Still, there's no denying that I've been tormented by the fact that my voice is not a physically practical thing. As poet Maya Angelou has noted, "There is no agony like bearing an untold story inside of you."

Truth.

To end that agony, writing became my voice.

Healing Dreams/Inner Voices

 Seven months—Found: her flip-flops

I found Jessica's purple flip-flops in a closet and broke down in tears.

With my finger, I traced the outline of her foot, molded into the footbed. Her foot still existed but as negative space.

I couldn't get enough of those shoes. I held them close.

I wanted to push them through the wall of my chest to a spot where they might fill up the emptiness.

My Head and My Heart

My thesis at Columbia was entitled "Growing Up Imperfect." It was about women with non-typical physical characteristics and how they had to grow up and live their lives in a world that prizes female perfection, how they survived and flourished within the limits of their ability to meet that standard.

Of course, it was journalism, so it wasn't about me. But I was obviously studying that subject for my own, very personal reasons: living with limits could be done and done well. I knew of people, women even—the ones I interviewed—who had done it.

Tellingly, I returned to a similar theme nearly thirty years later, as a Knight-Wallace journalism fellow at the University of Michigan. (That was my younger son Ben's freshman year there, 2001-02. He was finally leaving home and now his mother was coming with him! He stayed as far away from me as politely possible, producing perfectly plausible excuses for why we couldn't meet up.)

By this time, having lived my own life and created four others in the birthing of my children, my study was much more focused: "The Value of Limits: Disability in a Culture of Unlimited Possibilities." My timing seemed perfect as the national effort to sequence the human genome was nearing completion. I took classes at the medical school to consider the implications of genetic testing and manipulation, and at the law school to study the legal aspects of making those life-altering decisions for ourselves and our children.

At the heart of my studies was a question I wanted to be able to answer: If I could have chosen Jessica with all of her cognitive and neurological challenges, would I have?

This was a purely theoretical question, since no tests exist that would have predicted Jessica's disabilities. But it seemed crucial to consider since disability and disease and disappointment are ever present. And ultimately, our answers shape not only our families but our world.

A painful process of reckoning brought me to the realization that at age twenty-five, I would *not* have chosen Jess.

I have to sit with that for a moment because it startles even me.

But it's true. In fact, I thought twice about passing on my own disability, since stuttering tends to run in families and to occur most often in males. (Of course, my own case reflected neither of those conditions, so I figured chance must play a role.)

Parents today have more choice than ever about what kind of children they want to have, and that ability will only grow as science advances and genetic testing proliferates. We now have unparalleled ability to determine who gets born and who gets altered.

The question of whether to test and what to do with the results—What version of not-normal am I willing to live with?—will ultimately come to all of us, whether we want it or not. It may be there when we create life, but also when we decide whether and how to continue—or end—life.

To make the best choices, we need a clear picture of what life with a disability is like—the hard parts, certainly, but also the revelatory, happy parts, which too rarely get presented. The experience of families with disabled children and the insights of genetic counselors and others can impact whether people like Jess get born.

Which of the human traits that we consider detrimental should be fixed? Should short children be made taller? Should deaf children be made to hear? What about intelligence? How smart do you have to be to get to be born? Is going with the roll of the genetic dice irresponsible? If science allows us to avoid it, shouldn't we rescue our children from "disabling" conditions?

COVID-19 has reminded us that disability and

death are not distant specters but potentially imminent threats. Which of us will fall victim to this
virus, or the next one, and how will we respond to
the impact on our bodies? Which conditions can we
live with? What should we consider in deciding how
badly our lives can be compromised before pulling
the plug?

We need a deeper, lived-experience perspective
on what life with disabilities is like. A subgroup of
COVID-19 survivors may be permanently impacted.
How do they navigate their limits and what is society's role in helping them?

Beyond that, what is the value of having such
people in the world? What is the worth of disability in the absence of miraculous achievement
("overcoming") or obvious transforming impact
("inspiration")?

Life with Jess had provided me with a context
for considering the medical and scientific decisions
being made by researchers in the sanctity of their
labs, by politicians in the hallowed halls of government, and by individuals in deciding the best options
for their families. I figured I could put that context to
good use during my fellowship.

From a doctor's viewpoint, perfect health is the
ultimate ideal. Our views are conditioned by a society
that fears disability, sickness and dependence, so any
associated traits are to be avoided. That is why tests
exist, of course, and we make our decisions within
that social context.

That worries me because as advances in preventing imperfections grow, the range of what is considered acceptable narrows. Fewer potential people are good enough. Maybe people like Jess with cognitive, neurological and physical impairments won't make the cut. Maybe people like me.

We also need to determine exactly what we think disability is. We can or soon will be able to "correct" for susceptibility to disease, for example, but also for short stature, average intelligence and gender. Will our acceptance of what were heretofore considered quirks or characteristics be diminished? And if so, at what peril?

Is it better not to exist than to have a disability? Are there any benefits to having disabled people in the world?

In that regard, the statistics about testing for Down syndrome are troubling. Down syndrome is one of the least severe conditions that can be identified by prenatal testing. Increasingly, due to medical advances and educational opportunities, people with Down syndrome can live long, fulfilled lives.

Yet in the United States, 67 percent of parents who get a diagnosis of Down syndrome terminate the pregnancy, although that percentage swings depending on region of the country, as Sarah Zhang reported in her story, "The Last Children of Down Syndrome," in the December 2020 edition of *The Atlantic.*

Most parents who choose genetic testing are not seeking the perfect child, but a child as free from as many undesirable conditions and characteristics as possible. We humans have a profound aversion to risk and uncertainty, as Zhang noted. Yet becoming a parent is one of the riskiest things we do, sending us headlong into a lifetime of challenges and conditions that are unknowable and often beyond our control.

Individuals must decide whether to test, and what to do with the results, in the painful quiet of their own minds. But their singular choices are added to the decisions being made by people all over the globe. Ultimately, we will all have to live with what we've made.

After being Jessica's mom, I like to think I would step up to the experience of raising a child with a disability. I like to think that the knowledge and insight that come with lived experience would have opened my heart, stirred my courage and empowered me to embrace that challenging experience.

And if that opportunity arrived unbidden but undeniably mine, I like to think I would take it. (Indeed, I did take it.)

But what if I had a choice, what then? Would I choose a child with disabilities?

Once again I am stunned—at myself. Because I'm squirming to answer.

Ask me if I would have chosen Jessica, the person Jessica was, and hands-down, no question, I'm there, I'm her mom.

Then ask me if I would choose an unknown child-to-be with some missing chromosomes—when I could later choose a child without those potential deficits—and I'm not so sure.

But I *am* sure that I would now be capable of making that choice with an infinitely greater appreciation of the good that experience could bring. I would be able to envision a child who was more than a litany of atypical conditions and characteristics.

Zhang posed what for me is the fundamental question: What should parents value in their children?

I think of Jessica, who never brought home a stellar report card but deeply impressed a school bus driver simply by wishing him happy Thanksgiving.

I value that.

Preach—Encounters of the Disabling Kind

Given the world's proclivity for lists
- and bulleted items,
- these "Preach" interludes round up my thoughts in a linear fashion.

This one is about encountering people with disabilities, which should be no big deal but often is. I learned a lot about how to relate to people with disabilities from being one. And raising one.

But after just pouring my heart out about the larger implications of disability, I want to make sure you also have some practical guidelines for fully living with and embracing people with disabilities.

This information comes just in time, as we experience the aftermath of COVID-19, including the long-haulers, the people with long-term health conditions.

There are currently sixty-one million people with disabilities in the United States, and with COVID, as well as aging and medical advances, there will likely soon be many more.

If everyone knew the following, what a wonderful world it would be. Not perfect, but better.

First: Be present to the experience of interacting with someone who may not do things the way you do. Don't impose your abled perspective on someone who may look to be struggling but who is simply going about life with the body they've got. Just like you, only different. Think about when you're working with someone on a task they can perform much more efficiently than you, and they keep trying to take over, in effect *preventing* you from accomplishing anything. Good intentions are no excuse.

Second: Don't assume people with disabilities need your help. Generally, we don't. But when we do, we'll let you know. Eye contact can help determine if help is desired. Is the person engaging you? Are you engaging them? If the person can't see you, notice if they are acting with intent and proceeding at their own pace (not yours, this is key). Doing things with a disability can take what others consider "extra time." If, after thoughtful consideration, you determine someone might indeed need assistance, *ask*.

Third: Stop considering people with disabilities

brave or inspirational. This thinking leads to the bad behaviors outlined above. We don't feel nearly as depressed about ourselves as able-bodied people assume. More on this later, but guess what? The overwhelming majority of people with disabilities don't consider their "limits" to be the worst thing that ever happened to them. In fact, they marvel at the able-bodied world's tendency to put them on pedestals for simply living their lives. Often, we're more disabled by your ability-skewed perceptions than by our own bodies (or voices).

The late Lucy Grealy, author of *Autobiography of a Face*, was spot on when she noted that the saying "beauty's on the inside" is B.S. And she would know—her face underwent major changes due to the ravages of cancer. Rather than soothe the narrow-minded with such sayings, she counseled that we should instead expand the range of what we consider attractive.

So true. The problem is not the limits of the person whose face, or brain, or speech is nontypical, but the limits of the observer.

To my mind, the concept of being on the "autism spectrum" facilitates that expanded view but often only to the benefit of those on the higher end. With autism there is the bad, the not-so-bad, and the pretty darn good.

But the "bad" disability still exists—there's a hierarchy and those unable to speak are at the bottom—so the concept lets in only a lucky few. When describing their offspring, parents of children at the high end usually add, ". . . but she's high-functioning." Whenever possible, they include that qualifier. "My kid has autism/or any other disability that isn't cognitive, but she isn't stupid." Which, apparently, is the worst thing you can be.

As Jessica's mother that, of course, drives me bonkers. Our family friend Richard Prangley, the subject of my husband's book, *Waiting for Home: The Richard Prangley Story*, had to fight to overcome being labeled a "high-grade imbecile" in the 1950s. He was wrongly institutionalized for fifteen years—from age six to twenty-one—and had to do battle just to be allowed to contribute to our community. He eventually earned his right to be a taxpayer and worked for the state of Michigan for thirty years.

The 1927 United States Supreme Court decision in the case of Buck v. Bell also haunts me. Justices upheld a Virginia state statute requiring sterilization of the "unfit" (in this case young Carrie Buck, wrongly labeled a moron) "for the protection and health of the state." Such state laws were not struck down until the 1970s, the decade Jessica was born. That's how close this is.

But I digress. The above are general guidelines. Specific disabilities have their own parameters. I know about stuttering, so here are some tips, including those from my TEDx talk:

- Listeners—those disabled listeners I mentioned—are so caught up in their own discomfort when a stutterer is speaking that ending it is all they're thinking about. Everyone has stumbled and struggled to speak if only momentarily, and those painful moments come flooding back when listeners hear a stutterer. So, I feel for you, I do. But get over it.

- About one percent of the world's population stutters—more than seventy million people worldwide, including more than three million in the United States.

- Some five percent of all children go through a period of stuttering that lasts six months or more. Three-quarters of them will stop by late childhood. The rest become long-term stutterers.

- There is no cure for stuttering, but current treatments focus on a combination of goals designed to help people speak more easily and fluently, and to improve their understanding and acceptance of stuttering so that they don't see it as a limiting influence on their lives. Woven throughout treatment is a focus on helping people who stutter reduce their fears about speaking so that they can easily and effectively say what they want to say—stuttering or not.

- Experts think several factors contribute to stuttering, including genetics (sixty percent of the time it runs in families and four times as many males as females stutter) and neurophysiology—differences in the way people who stutter process speech and language. Researchers have identified three genes as a source of stuttering, which may eventually provide more insights.

- My stutter is my accent, so don't try to take it away from me by supplying the word I'm working to say. When you do that, you take away my power—so don't do it.

- And for Pete's sake, allow me the dignity of saying my own name. I confess to having a mean streak (just a little one) and when I'm trying to say my name—"Sh... Sh... Sh..." —and someone starts guessing—"Sheila, Sherry, Shelley, Shannon, Shirley, Shauna"— I can let my listeners go on guessing just for the entertainment value. What they come up with! Finally, I get it out. Hopefully, to avoid another session like that, they learn to just wait. Hopefully.

- President Biden takes a lot of jabs for his occasional non-sequitur speech patterns. As many stutterers will tell you, when we sense a problem word looming, we start figuring out if substituting the problem word is a good idea. When it seems we're more likely to lose listeners with the block than with a substitute word, we go for the latter, which can result in those unusual word sequences. Not exactly wrong but not on target,

either. When speaking, we stutterers are moni-
toring not only what we're saying, but how we're
saying it, and what that bodes for what we'll say
next. Yes, it's exhausting . . . .

- Stutterers don't suffer big-talkers gladly, largely
  because we're appalled by the sheer volume
  (as in, amount) of their output. Their nattering
  seems to create a soothing resonance within
  their own heads—but too often that's it. If you're
  contributing to the communication deluge of
  modern life, don't abuse language by using it
  just to make sound. Especially when there are
  other people struggling to be heard.
- Your ultimate challenge: make every one of your
  words count.

Here's the human toll that listeners' reactions
take, the core message of my TEDx Talk, so take note
if you see yourself:

*I've seen you wince when I'm speaking, look away
or actually break out in what I can only assume is
nervous laughter.*

*My real concern, however, is the point at which you
stop reacting to me and actually start listening. My
deepest fear is that you never do.*

*My stutter appears to take up your entire audi-
tory capacity. You ask me questions I've already
answered. Or you anxiously wait for me to stop*

talking—totally deaf to the meaning of my words—looking only to fill up the silence with the sound of your own fluent voice.

Why does my digression from the norm—which costs only seconds of your time—throw you so far off from your appointed role as listener when I'm the one speaking?

Stuttering has taught me much about listening. I need to pay attention to ensure that my responses—Every. Single. One.—are on point and as concise as I can manage. That has enabled me to have more direct connections precisely because verbal language challenges me. No wonder editing and molding words to their essential meaning has been my calling.

My model in all this is Deaf culture, which assumes that people cannot hear; therefore, those who are deaf are, in fact, not disabled. And another shocker: they don't want to be fixed. In part, that's because there's a Deaf gain in not being able to hear—an advantage that allows them to communicate in a more meaningful and intentional way because they cannot use verbal language.

The world has essentially forgotten how to listen; everyone just wants to talk. Anytime you're engaged in dialog with another person, remember: your silence is your gift to the conversation. What you have to say is secondary; it comes after the listening. Silence creates thinking time between words. It cultivates ideas still in the process of being formulated—both yours and your speaking partner's. Ultimately, silence is the oxygen for communication.

Healing Dreams/Inner Voices

 Ten months—I got out of the car

I had a *wonderful* dream of Jess last night.

We were hugging and I was pressing her into me because I was so glad to see her, and she was so glad to see me, and we just kind of melted together in the warmth.

Then the scene changed.

We were both in a car, but I had a sense of dread. I knew Jess was dead; something wasn't right.

So, I got out of the car.

Spirits and Aspirations

As you may have guessed, I believe in the power of the spirit, the soul, the subconscious, the unconscious, whatever you want to call it. We humans have an extra sense that simply has to be fostered. That belief has allowed me to write with the conviction of someone who thinks this missive may be her most valuable gift.

Having children can do that to you. You develop a sense of responsibility for what you've created that goes beyond providing food and shelter. You want to know that your offspring are skillfully, bravely, happily creating The Future.

At least that's how I explain what my father asked of me not long before he died in 1995. For the first and only time, he specifically asked me—his daughter, the journalist—to write something.

"Write about decency, about how it could change the world," he said.

Such was my father's belief in the power of words. And in the power of me.

At first his entreaty registered as an audacious request. "Egads, Dad, could you narrow it down?"

But ultimately, I heard it as a plea, a plaintive wish that was as simple as an old man's cry into a vast, cold night. And as complex as a father's wish for his child and his hope for the world because she lives there.

This from a man who had only one scrap of proof that he had had a childhood: a head-and-shoulders shot of a boy, perhaps six years old, with a big safety pin holding up one strap of his overalls. A man who worked in Detroit's auto plants before they became union shops, seeing them as a kind of nirvana after fleeing the coal mines of southwest Indiana. A man able to buy a brick bungalow in the suburbs (Roseville, Michigan) and put his children through orthodontia and college. A man, grown old, afraid to go to the grocery store before daylight on winter mornings because he knew the unscrupulous were waiting—he had read about it in the newspaper.

If we were all decent to one another, could we end childhood poverty, corporate greed, abuse by thugs? Probably not....

And yet he spoke with such conviction that I hesitated not to consider the possibility, let alone question that I could relay the message to the world in which he had invested all that was dearest to him—that being me, my sister, my brother, and ultimately his grandchildren.

My father was trying to ensure that he was among those perpetuating belief in the power of goodness in the world and in the promise of our children to manifest it.

No doubt my father would have believed that what I have to say is important, maybe even more important than Pulitzer Prize-finalist Joan Didion sitting down to write about her year of magical thinking.

My children are the audience that Joan did not have, and their reception is something I cannot do without. My children and I are linked in this telling; our common histories have brought us here and will ultimately impact who we are.

And then there's that *something* I have to give the world.

Unlike Joan, I love magical thinking—beyond the provable, beyond the familiar, into the uncharted territories of human consciousness. Nobody knows what's there, so the default position is to say nothing is there. But shouldn't we try harder to know?

Not all kids grow up as mine did with George the Ghost in the house. My mother first identified George, and he simply stayed. All of our home's strange and creepy noises could be attributed to George.

The picture falling from the wall, the door closing on its own, the floor creaking mysteriously. "That's just George." The unknowable was always present; it just was. It's true what poet Mary Oliver said about attentiveness, what she called the wisest and yet most preposterous thing she knew—that listening for the mysteries of the world can vastly expand your experience of it and that the soul is built entirely in that process.

As part of that attentiveness, I know—I have experienced, thanks to Jessica—that it's possible for someone to be gone but present. Those closest to us who have moved on still speak to us in whatever way we have prepared to hear them. For me it's contemplation, a focused listening that includes all of my senses. Sometimes it feels like prayer.

The trouble is that we don't prepare for that communication, so we can't tune in. Connecting is difficult, even with aids like religion, spirituality, science, transcendence, meditation. It takes conviction, which I suppose is a giving over to a kind of belief, a faith that what you're attempting is actually achievable.

All that's required is that you know what you believe. That's it.

But that means you have to find whatever lifts you to a place where you can see how crushing loss fits into your life. You have to get yourself above the loss, and you need a system for doing that.

Don't be lazy, don't get distracted. Your spiritual

life doesn't simply happen to you, just as you didn't learn to read by hanging around books or even people who could read. You had to do the work of learning yourself.

When my older son, Justin, took a textbook sales job in Dallas and became the first of my children to leave home, I thought I could assuage my fears for him by knowing that he had his belief system intact. I wrote a sappy card and asked him to actually tell me what he believed.

To his credit, Justin never told me I was out of my mind, although he never directly responded, either.

Today I know the answer: Justin's belief in his own goodness and power has made him a devoted husband and father. He is a case manager at a large law firm, guiding people through what is surely a most harrowing point in their lives. He is also a good writer, having started his career as a newspaper reporter. So maybe someday he'll write down his beliefs for me.

You really do need to name and articulate what you believe. That might sound uselessly abstract, but in fact it's the key to making your way in the world. How else would you know what to do, when to stay, when to go, when to turn? And by figuring out how you see the Big Picture, it's much easier to live well in the everyday Little Picture.

In the process of developing your spiritual life, you believe different things at different times, so you need to respect diversity in your own thoughts and in those of others. You need to be brave enough to stand close to someone who believes something different than you do. And you need to be ready to be wrong.

Above all, you need to apply critical thinking—you need to determine what you believe, but only after you've thoroughly questioned it. Beware of merely echoing someone else's thinking. Always take the time to ask: How did I come to believe this? Why do I believe it?

Your own experience is your best teacher. Get out into the world and see up close what's out there. This is key to avoiding rote, unthinking answers.

Your beliefs deserve respect and reverence. You should treat them that way, and you should seek out people who do likewise, even if they don't agree with you. This is the way the tribe, the nurturing community that saves us from isolation and desolation, is formed: people trusting one another with their beliefs and ultimately their dreams. It is holy ground.

I prize a church, an institution—a country, for that matter—that believes it can be better than it is. This is the most righteous aspect you can come from. Otherwise, hubris is a threat.

As hard as it is to find your own tribe, it's even more difficult to live with other tribes and to realize that theirs is holy ground, too. This is where respect for others is required in the name of peaceful coexistence.

I admire how the church/synagogue/mosque

serves as an organizing tool for finding the community of believers we want to proceed with.

I grew up in the Disciples of Christ Church—
Lakeside Christian Church in Roseville, Michigan,
in the 1960s—when it seemed from my early-teen
perspective that the church was a major force in
the world. The president of the United States was a
member (Lyndon Baines Johnson) and instrumental
in advancing the Civil Rights Act of 1964 and the
Voting Rights Act of 1965.

I met my first boyfriend, Ron, at a church youth
group event on April 9, 1969, and he was a pivotal,
prized influence in my life. Four years older and
active in political and social issues, he helped shape
my notions of the world and our place in it. He was
studying at Wayne State to be a teacher, worked as
an orderly at a hospital, and did draft counseling at
a priest's house in Detroit (which we believed was
under FBI surveillance). He loved rock and roll ...
and me.

Ron didn't end up being the one I'd make a life
with, but the life I did make was built on my founda-
tional relationship with him. The church was a big
part of that.

It would be very difficult to give important
moments in our lives heightened meaning if we
didn't create rituals around them, and our religious
communities provide that. Birth, marriage, death—
the ceremonies around these events acknowledge

that we, the actors, are sacred, somehow sanctified. (We need someone besides our mothers to assure us, "Blessed are you, holy are you.") To live without that recognition is to live a diminished life. And no life should go unrecognized—that is the bigger social imperative.

Believing is a deliberative process. It takes work to get there; you have to think about it, cultivate it. You don't just get anointed with it. The implications of what you do or fail to do with what you believe are enormous. I have come to realize this in a most profound and devastating way.

I don't know if my sister Jan was a religious/spiritual martyr or a delusional acolyte—you can be the judge as I tell her story—but I most definitely don't want my children among the martyred or misled. That's what makes the world dangerous.

Most people have no idea what they believe. Not that it keeps them from acting like they do. Examine the people with all the opinions. If you listen closely and go so far as to ask a question, you'll find that their arguments often fall apart. It's disappointing and disheartening because these people will sometimes be your friends.

When you speak, make sure what you say stands up to scrutiny. It won't always, of course, and then you'll be one of those disappointing people. But that's simply the signal that you need to work harder on formulating what you believe. You could spend your whole life on this, and it wouldn't be time wasted.

The world is not a safe place, but there is refuge in knowing what you believe. That certainty, as best as you can fathom it at any given time, is the essence of your power in the world. Knowing what you believe permits you to face great despair and immense pain with courage and grace. It allows you access to a spiritual aspect that can help you transcend the losses and limits you face. The most evolved people on the planet are there.

Many people spend little or no time trying to find this experience. Maybe it comes down to the work required. And the basic tools. If no one is pointing the way and the road is treacherous, alternate paths become more inviting.

You need to stay on the right path when you're formulating your beliefs, and this gets unbelievably tricky. There is no map, since the road you're forging—your path—is by definition uncharted, with divergent tracks that you must recognize to avoid becoming a zealot. And you definitely want to avoid the extremism propagated by the True Believers of anything. In your beliefs and in your politics, you want to allow room for argument.

The world is full of half-baked ideas put forth by people with little concern for outcomes beyond their own glorification. Those are easily dispensed with. But when thoughtful, kind people arrive at different conclusions from you on important issues, there must be room for them to act on their beliefs. You must establish a peaceful coexistence and allow your disagreements to continue.

The secret, then, is to find a place in what you believe that allows rational questioning and also spiritual exploration. I've heard it said that the fullest life resides in the uneasy space between the atheist scientist and the religious acolyte.

Ultimately, it may be of no consequence whether God invented humans or humans invented God. The fact is, to be happy every human being needs to find what brings them solace and hope, the keys to not merely surviving but leaving this world whole and fulfilled.

You do this not merely as an affirmation of your own life, but as encouragement to those watching you and looking for clues. We make our heroes in the same way and for a similar purpose: they help us survive.

You have the power to be happy. You have the power to be a beacon. What you believe answers essential questions about who you are and where you fit. Discovering those answers without God is difficult for me to imagine.

But you are not me, and I know God is a remote, mythological concept for many good people. I don't know what brings them solace and hope or how they will ultimately reconcile themselves with what life brings.

For me, happiness resides in finding all the signals and patterns in my experience of the world. It's not so much that God (or whoever) is sending me messages, as it is my power—which I've struggled mightily to cultivate—to derive insights from what has happened to me, the good and the bad.

Reading the world is a solitary experience, however. You don't have to see those lessons and, indeed, you don't even have to acknowledge that they are there. I simply contend that your world will be richer if you do.

Healing Dreams/Inner Voices

 One year—I cut her hair

In my dream last night, I had the exquisite pleasure of cutting Jessica's hair again. It's been so long.

I recognized the brassy, reddish-brown that August always colored it and the special places where it grew thicker.

It wasn't sad in any way—Jessica's hair was longer than she liked, so I needed to cut it. I wanted to cut it. And when I was done, she looked beautiful.

I only remember seeing her hair, but it was unmistakably Jess. I willingly lost my breath in the descent through her glorious hair, putting a kiss on her warm scalp and whispering, "Good-bye, good-bye."

Loss and Revelation—Jan

It's true that the magical thinking I just marveled about can, in fact, be dangerous.

I say that despite having used magical thinking to remain close to Jessica in my dreams. And in my life—especially when I found a notebook tucked in the cabinet where I keep the bills and important papers, several weeks after her death. Because it is my job to handle the business of our household, this cabinet was pretty much my enclave.

There it was, a notebook with my sister Jan's photo on the cover, attached with Jessica's trademark application of excess tape.

Inside were messages that my friends had sent to Jess after she had e-mailed them about Jan's death that February, just six months before Jessica herself would die. Jan had jumped from the Gorge Bridge that straddles the Rio Grande near Taos, New Mexico.

Jessica and Jan.

Theoretically she had jumped into water, but the cause of death was blunt-force trauma.

The words of comfort in that notebook were all neatly assembled for me to find—at that very moment, I believe. What went into their creation and what brought me to them is simply beyond my ability to comprehend. It could have been coincidence, happenstance, but then I wouldn't have those connections to Jess or to Jan. And I simply can't imagine choosing meaninglessness over meaning.

(The miraculous continued when I found a note Jessica had addressed to John and me and her siblings, which appears opposite this book's table of contents page. She apparently copied the words from the messages of sympathy I had received after Jan died. But when read after Jessica's own death, it seems a tender, heartbreaking good-bye.)

So, I am compelled to tell you about Jan, too.

Jan was the youngest of us three Emery siblings, all born in late May, all within three years of each other and all within ten days—Jan on May 21, Ralph, May 28, and me, May 30. (As young adults we chided our parents that they were "busy" during only one summer night in each of those three years.)

Jan and I shared a room upstairs in our family's brick bungalow, in the attic that had been converted into a bedroom, complete with rose and gray-colored tile, built-in bookcases, and a pink Princess phone.

Me, Jan and Ralph with our dad at Metropolitan Beach Metropark, on Lake St. Clair. (1957)

The tile was not only pretty, but it served a very practical purpose in helping delineate just where her side of the room started and mine ended. (The phone, atop the chest of drawers, was neutral territory, as was the black portable stereo with detachable speakers.)

Our mother made us matching dresses when we were little, but there are photos of us as older kids, when we could have objected, dressed in similar skort outfits, so we must have agreed to the match-up. We had the usual sister fights, but also consoled each other about our brother's slovenly eating habits when the family went out to dinner to celebrate good grades on our report cards. As young teens we also bonded mightily—we were in tears for several days—over a book about Annie Sullivan teaching Helen Keller to communicate.

We drifted apart over the years when I graduated high school and went to college. Reuniting became increasingly difficult. Things would start out fine, but our meetings would ultimately devolve into arguments that seemed to me to be about nothing. Jan would take offense at what I did, or what my boyfriend said or didn't say. She'd complain of neck pain from what she said was a playful jump into the Detroit River one night. Increasingly, she began to go her own way.

I'm not there yet, but I want to understand how my sister ended up dead in what should have been the prime of her life. The threads that led her to the bridge and then failed to hold and save her from the harrowing descent are intricately woven.

I start broadly: if we are lucky, we find friends and a life story that take us where we want to go. We formulate a blueprint for the project that is us and start building on it, connecting with the people and events that make for the whole, somewhere down the line. Incrementally, we put what happens to us into a context we can live with, one that allows us to move forward, no matter what. Somehow, we make sense of the chaos that is life.

But there is nothing simple or rote about the process, so anguish is unavoidable. There are times when our next move is unclear or when our past seems unworthy of our new, revised plan. And so, we struggle with what we see and with what we want to see as we attempt to mold our true selves from the unknown, which is possibility, and the known, which is past.

That is what I think is true, anyway.

What I know for sure is that my sister's body was found broken and lifeless, 660 feet beneath the Gorge Bridge on February 17, 2002. The police said she jumped, and I have no reason to believe that anything but her own volition, however tortured, was involved.

Still, I struggled fitfully to understand how a talented forty-six-year-old woman—whose friends said she was at an extraordinarily happy and fulfilling point in her life—could have ended up in a frigid chasm in February.

I know that each of us seeks to understand the essential design of who we are and to find an audience that appreciates it, be they our family, our co-workers, or our friends. We labor, in short, to reveal the value of the exquisite work of art that is us.

But how we go about doing that is as mysterious as any birthing process. And when the task culminates in self-destruction at mid-life, the inner workings that created that outcome are even more difficult to fathom. How does the design of a lifelong creation end in the destruction of that work of art? What is the artistic vision that makes that tenable?

It fell to my brother and me to find out.

We struggled with this realization for a few days, the time it took for the New Mexico State Police to get our sister's body out of the gorge. They were hampered by equipment problems and, we suspected, a lack of interest, for they had been called to recover another woman who was missing in the area—a woman who was lost, but alive.

Our parents, mercifully, were already dead. Our mother, just thirty-eight months prior; our father, almost six years before.

Ralph and I had to reconstruct not only our sister's death but her life. Not for nothing was Jan living 3,000 miles away in Santa Fe. She had long ago sought to distance herself from our Michigan-based family.

After studying massage therapy in London in the early 1980s, she lived in a succession of places that we figured were receptive to her trade: Hawaii, California and even Crete for a while. The last stop was Santa Fe in 1992, a place I want to believe really felt like home to her.

There is much more than vast physical distance between the Great Lakes and the desert, and I think she found solace in the stark contrast.

While we always had a post office box number for her, she purposely told us little of her life in the "Land of Enchantment," as a New Mexico license plate alluringly describes it. A few years before she died, Jan told us that her frustrating reticence was our punishment for never really listening when she shared the details of her life. She was angriest about us not understanding the chronic pain she said she suffered due to a neck injury in her early twenties, and the alternative healing she sought to ameliorate it.

It was true: we had never put those issues at the center of her life, we had never considered them definitive. But they were.

The plane carrying Ralph and me descended on the great unknown that lay in New Mexico on a cold, gray day. The landscape appeared desolate to us— barren and vast, the flat-topped mountains not so much beautiful backdrops but markers for the end of the world. They seemed even to have bruised the blue-black clouds that sat wounded above them.

We drove out of Santa Fe, up into the mountains toward Taos on a road that wound along the Rio Grande. The river flowed gently at this point, amid grasses struggling to be green at the promise of spring. Ralph was driving. I was trying to extract comfort from imagining this river—my sister's final destination—as peacefully nestled among the mountains.

But at the Rio Grande Gorge Bridge, I realized perspective is all. No comfort could be derived from this place that is a violent gash in the earth.

Ralph and I parked in the visitor lot where Jan just days earlier had left her car, the 1992 Ford Taurus that had been my mother's. We saw the signs (did she notice them?) warning that the state of New Mexico was not responsible for any injuries or losses incurred at this place.

We started to walk out onto the bridge with some other tourists and came upon a woman frozen in place, clinging to the railing. She said she was terrified of heights and had to stop there. Her braver family had gone ahead to see the breathtaking view.

We commiserated with her and then inched onward. There is something defiant about making your way along this bridge. Were it not for this edifice, human beings would never see the violent vista of this place that seems to tug threateningly should you dare to look it in the eye from this vantage point.

*Ralph at the Rio Grande Gorge Bridge,
and later sitting on the walkway when he
could go no farther.*

Ralph grew increasingly uneasy, choosing to walk in the road where cars zoomed by, rather than closer to that terrifying brink, even though there was a walkway and a sturdy railing. Soon he said he could go no farther. He handed his camera to me. We had come to record the spot where we thought our sister went over.

"Take a picture for me," he said, sitting down on the curb, his back to the assaultive gorge, his feet in the road.

My own footing was precarious enough that the act of juggling two cameras seemed threatening. I stopped and worked to find my balance with the added accouterment. Okay, I assured myself, there it is, I've got my bearings.

I continued on the bridge, the brutal February wind whipping me. Each step I took became an angry march into that place that had swallowed up my sister, sucked her whole into its vortex, tore and smashed her body, and refused to give her up for two days.

I pushed myself to go on and finally reached the point above the gorge where the Rio Grande flows beneath, the likely point where Jan had jumped with the help of a plastic milk crate. I had stolen only side glances at the gorge up until now, struggling to maintain my balance and my composure. So, I stopped, and turning without lifting my feet, faced the ragged void.

It was beautiful, but also horrific: the extraordinarily steep descent, dizzying; the ragged rocks,

The spot on the bridge where I think my sister went off.

menacing. What I feared most was that nanosecond that could transform the beauty of this place into a bludgeoning, which I imagined happened with my sister.

The angry tears came as I cried into the wind, "You fucking gorge! You horrible, fucking gorge!"

But the gorge wouldn't yield to human action; my words were carried off by the unrelenting wind. I stood howling and insignificant above the enormous breech.

The next day, when Ralph and I arrived at the state Office of the Medical Investigator in Albuquerque and explained that we were there regarding Jan Emery, the receptionist couldn't find her name on the registry. We insisted that our sister's body was indeed there, and so she looked again into the computer screen, tapping nervously at the keys that both promised and threatened to reveal what was inside.

"Oh, you mean 'Woman Found in Gorge'," she said, reading from the list. "Yes, she's here."

In the local newspapers Jan had been the "Woman Found in Gorge" for several days. The stories noted that a car owned by Janice G. Emery was found at the bridge, but the body and the name had yet to be definitively connected. That, in part, was why we were there.

It was a relief to learn that families coming face-to-face with the bodies of their dead relatives is the stuff of TV dramas, not real life, not real death. All they needed from us was a current photo, preferably two, front and side view, to identify her. She wasn't too badly banged up, they said. Not bad enough to be maimed, just dead. Still, that was not the last memory we wanted of our sister; we let the photo provide confirmation.

The medical investigator told us that people jumping from such a height die immediately. They suffer a heart attack on the way down, or they lose consciousness, or go into shock. We wondered if he was just trying to comfort us, to convince us that our sister didn't actually feel the impact that had broken her body.

In fact, Jan's insides had likely been violently torn apart in her leap—her spleen, lungs, and heart shredded by her broken ribs, her backbone snapped, her liver ruptured.

That's what Tad Friend found in researching a story for *The New Yorker* ("Jumpers," October 13, 2003) about people who leap off the Golden Gate Bridge. Jumpers tend to idealize what will happen after they step off the bridge, Friend wrote, "But the impact is not clean." A Coast Guard officer he quoted compared it to taking an egg-beater to someone's organs.

Connecting an identity to the body at the bottom of the gorge became even more difficult when we finally got a court order to open the storage locker that had become a kind of tomb, a repository for all the evidence of who Jan was. Among the clues: court petitions to change her name to Janiah Aranha.

I searched for some significance in the name. But I knew that unlike most naming processes, which look back to previous generations, this one must have looked forward to a state of mind that I was only beginning to unravel. There was no memory to this name; it was anticipatory. But who, exactly, was our sister expecting to become?

From the documents, it looked as if she had gone through the necessary legal steps but had not completed the name change. The process appeared to have been under way for months, perhaps years, before she jumped. And it had taken some doing.

First, she had to petition the court for a waiver of the usual fees. On the application, she listed her residence with her post office box address, G63. Didn't that seem strange to court officials? On the "expenses" page for listing rent costs, she put $0. Did anyone wonder about that? Under "entire family income" she put $0. Under assets she listed a car worth $300.

The date on the document was December 16, 1998, six days after the death of our mother, who had been in fragile health. Jan missed the funeral. She was on a camping trip and out of cell phone range, so we couldn't reach her. Had she received our messages before filling out the document?

The medical examiner asked if we wanted the clothes Jan was wearing. No, but the inventory was puzzling: three shirts, two sweaters, one coat, two pairs of pants, three pairs of socks, a pair of shoes, one neck warmer and one pair of gloves. No I.D. or car keys, but $110 in cash—two fives and a one-hundred-dollar bill.

There were a couple of theories about what she took with her when she jumped. One, that she probably contemplated the jump for quite a while at the gorge before actually doing it, and needed the clothes to keep her warm in the dark morning of the new moon.

The other was that she planned to fly off from that brink and needed the change of clothes and cash for use in another dimension.

The latter explanation opened a perspective on our sister that scared my brother and me. It made our sister look crazy.

Jan's friends in her co-housing community had been in touch with us by phone since the beginning of the ordeal, grieving with us and offering to help in any way they could. Ralph and I didn't know what to make of these people we had never met, people now connected to us via our estranged sister who was no longer alive. What role did they have in her life? What did they know about her death?

Healing Dreams/Inner Voices

 Thirteen months—My friends scare her

I dreamed I was talking with my friends Sarah and Judy when I suddenly realized Jess was also there. I was amazed!

But she was about ten years old, not the twenty-five-year-old woman who had left us more than a year before.

Stunned to see her in any form, I struggled to find the breath to tell Sarah and Judy, "Look, she's here!"

But they couldn't hear me.

I reached out to Jess in awe and rapture. Maybe even desperation.

But Jess recoiled. She was afraid of us.

Jan, cont.

J an's friends insisted that we come to see them, and so we did.

My senses were on overload and high alert. Jen, one of Jan's neighbors in the housing co-op, invited us to her home to meet some of Jan's other neighbors and friends. A young woman with a husband and two small children, Jen said she was a good friend of Jan's and had been taking lessons from her in the teachings of Carlos Castaneda.

Castaneda plays a major role in this story, so by way of background: Castaneda was born in Peru and earned his doctorate in anthropology in 1973 from the University of California, Los Angeles. Starting with *The Teachings of Don Juan* in 1968, he wrote a series of books that describe his experience studying the ancient religious practice of shamanism under don Juan Matus, whom he described as a Yaqui sorcerer.

Castaneda's website (Castaneda.com) says don Juan Matus taught Castaneda "everything he knew about energy, how to cultivate it within ourselves and then use it in our everyday lives. [Castaneda's] 12 books have sold more than 28 million copies in 17 languages and have become the source for helping millions of people manifest the life of their dreams, by bringing the once closely held knowledge and wisdom of the Toltec shamans to anyone who desires an extraordinary life."

Scholars and critics have debated whether Castaneda's work is fiction, but supporters insist his books are either true or at least valuable works of philosophy.

Castaneda founded Cleargreen, a California-based organization that promotes Tensegrity, which Castaneda described as the modern version of "magical passes." As explained on the back cover of Castaneda's *Magical Passes: The Practical Wisdom of the Shamans of Ancient Mexico*:

> *For us to perceive any of the worlds that exist beside our own, not only do we have to covet them but we need to have sufficient energy to seize them. In this revolutionary book, Carlos Castaneda offers readers the key to this energetic conditioning for the first time, revealing a series of body positions and physical movements that enabled various sorcerers, and their apprentices, to navigate their own sorceric journeys.*

Castaneda withdrew from public view in 1973, living in a large house in Westwood, California, with three female colleagues until his death in 1998 from liver cancer at age 72.

All that is more than I knew on the day Jen told others in the housing group that we would be there. They came to see Ralph and me, touchingly saddened by our sister's passing. It seemed each of them emanated a piece of the now broken mosaic that was our sister: the intellect, the emotion, the remoteness, the creativity, the wariness, the desire to connect.

I loved them for having loved my sister in a way Jan wanted to reciprocate. I was never able to achieve that. I was overwhelmed. I cried. They cried with me.

Jen, especially, was adamant that Jan did not jump to end something, but to *begin* something. I wanted to believe that, but what was that "something"?

A few days later, a reporter for *the Santa Fe New Mexican* began to assemble the facts for an article published on February 20, 2002. I'm not sure why she dug so deeply into my sister's death. Like many spectacular bridges, the Gorge Bridge has long been a magnet for jumpers. But I'm forever grateful that she did.

Friends: Woman's death not suicide
By Marissa Stone

Janice Emery apparently hoped she could fly like a bird.

And sometime between Feb. 12 and Thursday (Feb. 14), she might have tried to find out whether she could. Police said Emery jumped off the Rio Grande Gorge Bridge near Taos.

A few days before Emery left her Santa Fe house, she told a neighbor that women who studied with the mystic Carlos Castaneda would go with their teacher to a place in Mexico many years ago that they would jump from. One of the women, sometimes referred to as a witch, jumped with Castaneda, Emery told her friend. The friend couldn't say what happened to the witch, but Castaneda "woke up in his office in Los Angeles."

"I said, 'Jan, you're not planning on jumping?'" Jennifer Railey asked her friend incredulously. "'On flying?'" Railey was also a neighbor and spiritual student of Emery's.

"That woman was not suicidal," Railey said. "We can't understand what her path was, but her intention was not to kill herself."

But Emery told Railey, "I could (mess) up and do something stupid, get myself killed, but that's not my intention. Even though I'm your teacher, don't put me on a pedestal. All humans are subject to mistakes."

Emery had been a student of Castaneda, a man who wrote several books of mystical experiences with a Mexican shaman whom he called Don Juan. Emery told people she believed in changing her perception of reality through meditation and out-of-body experiences that allowed her to move her spirit from place to place at will.

On Feb. 14, authorities found the 47-year-old Santa Fe woman's Ford Taurus abandoned near the Rio Grande Gorge in Taos. On the gorge bridge, 660 feet above the Rio Grande, a patrolman found a plastic milk crate propped up against the railing. Authorities feared Emery used it to "help herself over the bridge."

A day later, a search-and-rescue crew spotted the dead body of a woman in the river about a mile and a half south of the bridge. On Sunday (Feb. 17), state police hired Known World Guides of Taos to help bring the body out of the water with a raft. The state Office of the Medical Investigator, using a photo of Emery, confirmed the identity.

Emery's friends and neighbors, who listened to and respected her spiritual beliefs but did not embrace them, said they are "shocked" by her death. None of them believed she intended to harm herself.

"I think she was really thinking she could fly off," said Elisabeth Sherif, a friend and neighbor of Emery's at their co-housing community on West Alameda Street.

"Jan's belief was that we didn't have to leave this plane with our body left behind," Railey said. "That we are magical enough to take our bodies with us when we go—as the ancients in Mexico taught."

"But she was very grounded," said Sondra Kosel. "It's hard to imagine her taking that kind of a risk."

Friends referred to Emery as practical, sensible, disciplined, down-to-earth and a good listener.

"She wasn't airy fairy," Kosel said.

Emery, originally from Michigan, was happy and bouncy, a friend Caroline Lippincott said. "She noticed everything ... the beautiful day, the clouds."

Emery's abilities, which included jewelry making, woodworking and scuba diving, were many. She was a masseuse, a healer and a teacher of Castaneda's spirituality. Emery loved the outdoors and would take friends on long hikes, Lippincott said.

But Emery also had a head injury brought on by cancer that probably led her to study healing in England and California. In her studies, she met Castaneda, who died in 1998.

"I think she wanted to be with Castaneda's people and her injuries drove her to this path that kind of saved her but at the same time removed her from this reality," Lippincott said.

The last time friends saw Emery was the morning of Feb. 12.

"I saw her light go out at around 4 a.m.," said Sherif, who lived next door.

Emery told friends and neighbors that week she was going to Michigan to take over a friend's massage business and would return in April. She left behind a "bogus" phone number where she could be reached, Sherif said.

Emery also told Railey that her trip to Michigan was "so much more. You just don't understand."

"I think she might have not wanted to tell people and went to experience (flying)," said Lippincott.

Before Emery left, she left gifts for her friends, including a large micaceous clay pot for posole she gave Sherif. She also made a terracotta goddess for Railey.

Emery also marked the pages of Castaneda's book "The Wheel of Time" for Railey with blue Post-It notes: "Whenever a warrior decides to do something, he must go all the way, but he must take responsibility for what he does. No matter what he does, he must know first why he is doing it, and then he must proceed with his actions without having doubts or remorse about them."

"And that's what she did," Railey said.

Truly understanding Jan's motivations is, of course, impossible without her here to explain them. I have tried not to torment myself in that search. A part of me wants to come to peace with it, as Jan's friend Jen seemed to.

But I can also get angry thinking about Castaneda's so-called freedom from personal history. It apparently allowed him to make up things about himself and required his followers to erase their former lives, including connections to family.

Maybe that's what Jan was trying to do with the name change—purge herself of herself, which she had come to see as a false cultural construction. Maybe she felt she had to become an empty vessel so that the spirit of whatever she was seeking could come through. But maybe that emptiness overwhelmed her.

I have to make do with maybes.

Months later, in going through the few things Jan had stored in preparation for her next move, I found the following narrative atop a stack of typed and handwritten pages that comprised a book she was writing. It appears to describe her efforts to come to grips with the logistics of jumping into the gorge. To me, it is a scripted nightmare.

Two lights in Espanola (N.M.) stayed red. Had to go through red lights. Red light in side rearview mirror as I entered the rest stop in the morning. Dogs barking (2). Distracting—I went back twice. Wasn't oriented properly in the dark.

Stood on ledge. Couldn't do it. Voice in head said, "Go sit down and a have a cup of coffee."

Went back to pee and didn't recognize my own hands.

Saw a luminous being at the car to my left and near the back end of my car. Could only see it from the corner of my eye.

As I drove away, I saw a rabbit cross the road from left to right. A field mouse followed closely behind him. Scared as a rabbit. Timid as a mouse.

Went to McDonald's to have coffee. Saw newspaper of suicide of Daniel Sogen.

Drove back to Santa Fe. Saw Caroline. She didn't see me despite my honks and horrors. Followed her to Bill's house. "That's horrible." She goes to art class.

I drive to storage (unit) and get blankets, then drive to rest area outside Santa Fe. Sleep one hour. Decide to try crate in truck as a step stool. Decide to go to Taos to try again.

In Taos I get more familiar with the area. Try to feel more comfortable.

Drive westward during magnificent slow sunset.

After sunset I take crate out and experiment with jumping over rail.

Go back to SF rest area. On the way I see two cats who cross my headlight beam from right to left.

Second cat gets startled by my lights and freezes.
I don't hit either one.

Up at 3 p.m. Get coffee and juice. Go to Chavez
Center. Cop comes up to car to investigate. I tell him
I'm just waiting for it to open.

Have shower. Feel good. Do movements "on stage"
and on floor of large room that looks like gorge.

The logistics and resolve stunned me. My sister was plotting her own death, not with despair but precision. It seemed a singular horror story.

But Matthew Dickman's poem "Trouble," from his book *All-American Poem*, reminded me that self-destruction is repeated with regularity and even included his brother among its victims (death by fentanyl patch).

The poet recounts the deaths by suicide of some twenty people, among them: Marilyn Monroe, Marlon Brando's daughter, Bing Crosby's sons, Ernest Hemingway, Hemingway's granddaughter, Hart Crane, John Berryman, Virginia Woolf. And Larry Walters, who shot himself after having won renown for ascending 16,000 feet in a lawn chair born aloft by helium balloons.

I found unexpected comfort in the seeming ubiquity of such tragedy. My sister's demise was not as singular as I had imagined. And my experience as her survivor was not unique—we were all dealing with mysteries that likely would remain that way.

Found among Jan's papers, a photo that seems to show her assuming a take-off position.

I wrote my own verse (no poetry, just the crush of feeling) to add to the poet's litany:

My sister stood in the frigid wind
for hours
before determining .... What,
exactly? That she was too
depressed
to live? The circumstances
don't seem to bear that
out. I think
she thought
she could fly. Science
calls that delusion
(schizophrenia?), I guess. When does
magical thinking
become dangerous? Am I
in danger
of becoming
dangerous?

Healing Dreams/Inner Voices

 Fifteen months—I watch her survive

I dreamed I saw Jess sink below the surface in a swimming pool. I was underwater myself and watched someone else pull her up.

There was no panic involved—just a momentary scare. (Is tragedy that random? Is our grasp on happiness that tenuous?)

Jess got out of the pool and threw up, as she did when we were trying to revive her on the beach when she drowned. Only this time, my main concern was the smell of her breath, not its existence.

I wanted to find her some water and mints so she would be embraced by the other people at the pool when she returned to share her story.

Jan, concluded

It took me nineteen years to get to all the pages beneath the one that detailed Jan's journey on that last day. The pages weren't numbered—of course they weren't, Jan didn't work that way—so I had to piece together their sequence by typewriter font and type of paper, in addition to what I could make of the chronology.

What I found was a story much more intricate, much more tightly woven than I had imagined.

Maybe Jan *did* expect to end up somewhere other than the bottom of the gorge when she jumped.

Robert Marshall, writing in *Salon* ("The dark legacy of Carlos Castaneda," April 12, 2007), mentioned Jan's leap and noted the allure of entering what Castaneda called the nagual, a state of awareness that allowed followers to experience an alternate dimension of reality. The promise of this experience may have been based on a scene Castaneda told in varying versions, in which he jumps from a cliff into the nagual.

Marshall quoted Castaneda's description of the event from Castaneda's 1984 book, *The Fire from Within*: "I didn't die at the bottom of that gorge—and neither did the other apprentices who had jumped at an earlier time—because we never reached it; all of us, under the impact of such a tremendous and incomprehensible act as jumping to our deaths, moved our assemblage points and assembled other worlds."

Castaneda said that if you mastered the right skills, you could avoid death and instead control when and how you left the Earth—vanishing completely, as if you never existed.

My mind was reeling: cut off from family and personal ties and immersed in a new way of being in the world, perhaps someone could start believing they weren't like most people on Earth.

Maybe the magical thinking that had led my grandfather to become a priest (more on that later) and me to become—what? A deep thinker? A mystic with one foot on the ground? A searcher of something that turned out to be attainable?—had instead been my sister's undoing.

To find the answer I had to make my way through the maze Jan had left in her stack of papers, her book. I discovered that Jan's neck injury and her quest to heal it were indeed the center of her life. For more than twenty years.

She wrote about a late-night swim in the Detroit River after drinking with her date in the summer of 1977, when she was twenty-two. A swift current caused something to "snap in my shoulder and what felt like a bolt of lightning exploded in my head. . . . The next morning, I awakened in great pain. . . . I could hardly move my neck and something was wrong with the alignment of my left eye. . . . It seems stupid and tragic to me now that I did not seek medical attention at the time. But I deeply and desperately believed that I had to take care of myself no matter how badly I felt. To seek medical assistance would be expensive and bring unwanted attention to myself. It would be just another example of how bothersome I could be. I did not want to appear weak to anyone, and if I made a big deal out of this, I would end up missing work and jeopardize my employment. If I mentally ignored my pain, it would go away."

My sister sounds almost determinedly alone in that passage.

This was the summer Jessica was born. I don't remember Jan mentioning the injury at that time, although John and I were living about two hours away in East Lansing. Maybe I wasn't paying enough attention. I do remember our mother had recently suffered a mild heart attack and was unable to help me as a new mom and perhaps my sister.

Jan had studied film and theater at Wayne State University, but in the early 1980s she moved to London to study massage therapy. It seemed like an impulsive decision, but now I think she may have been trying to find help for her condition.

In 1982, she enrolled at the Gerda Boyesen Institute in Acton Park and began studying psychology, psychotherapy, and massage with Boyesen. (Jan also wrote that she worked at the Institute as a receptionist, seamstress, typist, janitor, massage therapist, and babysitter, so I imagine a good part of her life was centered there.)

Boyesen (1922-2005) had studied psychology in Oslo and trained as a physiotherapist (physical therapist). She is credited with originating biodynamic psychology (a form of body psychotherapy) and identifying a bodily function she called psycho-peristalsis, by which the gastro-intestinal tract not only processes food but also stress, life experiences, and emotional and psychological events.

As Jan described it, Boyesen "recognized that the structures we develop in our mental patterning are in part responsible for our individual ways of being in the world. . . . She believed that the body, in the intestinal action of peristalsis, could dissolve that basic patterning."

I think that's what Jan was describing when she wrote that during the winter of 1985, "I began the work of healing my neck and head injury, and I kept at it each day for the next thirteen years. Almost always the pressure inside my head was so great I could not fall asleep until I had spent sufficient time—at least two hours—dissolving the tissue that was causing the constriction in my head, neck and face and relieve the uncomfortable, sometimes incapacitating pressure. . . . I could easily spend eight hours a day focusing on and dissolving tissue."

I remember Jan talking about this on her infrequent visits and thinking it was a mysterious ailment that she was trying to remedy with a mysterious treatment. But I really didn't know enough about either to accurately make that judgment. I didn't recognize my ignorance.

I had things to do. My third child, Ben, was born in 1983, Jessica was showing more significant developmental delays, and I was trying to maintain a semblance of my career by teaching journalism at MSU and publishing books of John's newspaper columns about our family, *Kin* and *Kin, Too.*

Meanwhile, Jan was making life-changing acquaintances while at the Gerda Boyesen Institute. It was during this time that Jan met Avraham, "Avi," whom she described as a healer proficient in reflexology, a form of alternative medicine involving the application of pressure to specific points on the feet and hands.

Jan wrote moving descriptions of Avi's tremendous impact on her: "Meeting Avraham was one of the best things that ever happened in my life."

Avi counseled her on many things, she wrote, including the potentially debilitating aspects of sexual relations and masturbation, and the constriction caused by wearing panties and bras. They were the same age, both born in 1955, but Jan did not describe any sexual relationship between them.

She wrote that Avi was also an "aficionado" of Castaneda and admired him for living the life Castaneda prescribed. Avi encouraged Jan to read Castaneda's books, which clearly altered the course of her life.

"I am acutely aware of the fact that I would not be alive today if it were not for the work of Carlos Castaneda," Jan wrote years later in her book. "His books came into my life at a time when my life force could no longer sustain itself without the input of a radical new way of thinking and acting in the world. I desperately needed a new kind of structure, fluid and expansive. More than anything though, I needed validation of the magical. That validation came in the form of the life lived and shown to me by Avraham, a healer from Haifa, Israel."

(It seems at this point Jan did not trust her own magical thinking and so was looking for affirmation from people like Avi, people far enough along on the spiritual journey to know what they were doing. Near the end of her life, she was confident enough to go it alone. That solitary pursuit may have made her quest lethal.)

Over the years Jan and Avi had apparently lost touch. In a letter to him dated November 16, 2001, just three months before she died, Jan said she had found his address via his website.

She told him: "My accomplishments over the past

fifteen years have been few and can be listed simply: I managed to stay alive thanks to you and Carlos. I learned a lot about healing and becoming more aware because death was and continues to be my best and wisest friend. (Ah, I can feel it breathing down my neck at this very moment.) I stayed on the path of the spirit as best I could. In return it revealed to me a task that now consumes every moment of my existence. That task is, of course, just a small part of a much, much larger purpose that swallows us all if we are lucky."

As best I can understand, Jan had determined after decades of searching that her purpose was to help elevate the consciousness of large numbers of people. She thought this could be accomplished by altering their assemblage points, which she believed are at the center of the human electromagnetic field and are responsible for interpreting (assembling) the reality we perceive. Moving the assemblage points of many people would be brought about by gathering them in theaters and transporting their consciousness via film.

(I told you it was complicated. . . .)

Jan wrote that her book was meant to describe for a larger audience "new energetic possibilities in the world. One of these is the opportunity for large numbers of people to experience unprecedented energetic phenomena through the film medium."

She believed her partner in this work was the actor/director Robert Redford. Jan came to this realization over the course of more than two decades, starting with a voice at a movie theater while watching *The Great Gatsby* in 1974, telling her she would marry the man on the screen.

Jan believed she had experienced the altering of her own assemblage points in 1993, watching Redford in the film *Indecent Proposal* in a theater.

In a 1998 letter to Redford that she included in her book, Jan explained: "What I actually experienced—though you never asked—was a sudden state of complete perceptual blankness, the ultimate Zen experience. . . . After considerable effort I was able to recall the last thing I was aware of before entering the land of nothingness. You, as the character John, were explaining how you had seen a young woman on a train thirty years earlier and always regretted not having the courage to approach her. You were determined nothing like that would happen again. Then I was gone. When I returned I 'knew' two things. One was that my assemblage point had moved, and the other was that its movement had something to do with the relationship between me and the man on screen, my counterpart."

She wrote to Redford, "You were the man I had encountered in several out-of-body experiences ... actually, there are many other connections but they are too numerous to discuss here."

One of these connections occurred in 1991, at the Phoenix Bookstore in Santa Monica, where Jan had gone to see Deepak Chopra. There she saw a man dressed all in black who "had something extra" about him, an "unusual configuration." Jan said the man was Robert Redford. She wrote that she had a "revelation" while driving home on the 405 freeway that this was the man she had been looking for, her counterpart.

In the 1998 letter, she explained to Redford that the Phoenix Bookstore was considered a meeting place for those involved in ushering in a new era. Carol Tiggs, Castaneda's counterpart, had "reentered" the world there in 1985, after apparently disappearing just as improbably from a hotel room in Mexico ten years earlier while with Castaneda.

Jan made several efforts to reach Redford through letters, explaining the plan and urging him to quit resisting what she considered his destiny. Finally, she realized that he would not be her counterpart and that she would have to accomplish her task alone.

"If our species is to have a future at all, man must become aware of his energy essence and how to live as an energy being," she told Redford in the 1998 letter. "I believe that awareness must come within the next generation and that the knowledge must reach an enormous number of people. Film is a perfect tool for achieving that."

She was even moved to chastise him for failing to respond: "I feel reluctant to give you this information because I do not believe you have earned it. Fortunately for the rest of the world, the Spirit doesn't give a damn what I think. My duty and purpose is to merge with the intent of something that is far greater than me or you. For reasons I do not fully understand, and even though you have missed the first act altogether, the spotlight is still on your mark. All you have to do is lose yourself and step into it."

He never did. Which seemingly brought her to write the 2001 letter to Avi. Apparently Avi had a role to play:

"... I am writing to you as one who is linked to another by fate. I suspect the time has arrived for those of us who share similar energetic configurations and are on the same path to come together to consciously form one intent toward fulfilling a common but enormous task.... My piece reveals the very real possibility of being able to move the assemblage points of many hundreds and perhaps thousands of people at exactly the same time. The spirit has showed me in a general way how that can be accomplished and who may be involved in such an enterprise. . . . But first we must all come together."

There is no indication if the letter was ever sent or if Avi ever responded.

I struggle with the fundamental question: Did she mean to end her life with the jump? Or plan to reassemble it after?

"It is believed that each human being is capable of expanding his or her awareness to include the possibility of existing as an energetic being," Jan wrote in her book. "Such a step necessitates revolutionary changes in individual perception—from seeing ourselves as physical beings to perceiving ourselves as energetic beings, a 180-degree shift in awareness.

"The energy body, which is separate from the physical body, must be strong enough to sustain the perception of the physical body without collapsing or being drawn back into it. If the energy body can sustain the view of the physical body long enough, the empty mass of physicality begins to dissolve or disintegrate and the energy is totally absorbed by the energy body, sucked up as it were into the black hole of perception. In order to reassemble the physical body, the energy body must intend the stream of time to which the physical body belongs and is energetically attuned."

This thinking was obviously built on Castaneda's teachings, but Jan was no blind acolyte. In her book she chafed at his authoritarianism and recognized his limitations. She was especially dismissive of the high fees charged for Tensegrity seminars, which she actually complained to Cleargreen about.

She wrote at one point, "The challenge is not to be intimidated by either Carlos or Carol. It is necessary that all of us work together in the world at the same time. There is no authority, only the Eagle's command, the dictates from energy itself. He is bound by his duty and I am bound to mine. I can learn from his teachings but I cannot be guided by his intent. My duty is not to him. The idea of mass ignition did not arrive with the ancient or the modern sorcerers. It came from the emanations at large, which dominate our time."

While acknowledging her own limits—including questioning her ability to be a world-changer, which haunted her even as she wrote that final entry in her book—she started positioning herself for a leadership role in that process.

Maybe this is the point at which magical thinking becomes dangerous.

After her supposed counterpart and guides—Carlos, Robert and perhaps, Avi—had failed to perform, Jan appeared ready to do the work alone. She would become the nagual, the leader the people of the world needed to take them to a new level of awareness.

With Tiggs's return to Earth, "The old rule ended at that point in January 1985," Jan wrote in her book. "Unbeknownst to either Carlos or Carol, a new rule was being formed. That rule stated that the new woman nagual was to stay in the world alone. She was commanded to find the new nagual man on her own, using only the published teachings of the old nagual (Carlos). She did not come into direct contact with Carlos until 1995, and then they did not speak directly.

"The new nagual woman (Janice) did indeed accomplish her task," Jan wrote. "She intuited the command to find her counterpart. She found the new nagual man (Robert) at the same place the old nagual woman found her counterpart, namely, the Phoenix Bookstore. The task of finding Robert necessarily included the discovery of their joint task, bringing the rest of the world into another world.

"Robert was also looking for his counterpart," Jan continued in her book. "The force of that act reached Janice and through it she was able to confirm the nature of their joint task. Robert intuited the joint task but not as specifically as Janice did. Since Robert was positioned prominently in the world, he was able to fulfill his task only in part."

The words I wrote in a previous chapter come to mind: we interpret what happens to us so that we can survive in the world. Jan was actively doing that, right up until the end.

Sometimes we are right.

And, sometimes, we are wrong.

"Total validation never comes," Jan concluded at one point in her book. "There is always a part of the story left untold."

And so it is with Jan's story... and perhaps my own.

Still, I have much in common with my sister, even at this late date in terms of our mutual existence in the world. Jan said the purpose of the book she was trying to write " ... is to describe as well as I can the moments in my life that have the most magical significance. These are the moments that have motivated me to pursue an alternate path and caused me to change the course of my life again and again.

"When taken together, they describe an underlying current that runs through my life. This current is a story in itself and leads into another world. When the force of that current bubbles up into everyday experience, there is a resultant incongruity, a dissonance that shatters my expectations of life and forces a new perspective.

"The purpose of my life is to bring this current into actuality. The power of the story can, I believe, help to propel not only my life but also the world into a magical modality. Everyone has a story. This is mine."

Those last few words are essentially the same words, the same sentiment, even the same cadence I used in the first chapter of this book, long before I had read hers.

Jan and I may never have been closer.

Healing Dreams/Inner Voices

 Seventeen months—Exhaling happiness

I've been trying to move from living through grief to living with loss.

Breathing is still my little ritual.

It's as if I am unable to breathe deeply and hold it— to fill my lungs fully with all the "vapors" of living.

It's impossible because there are holes in me now.

And happiness, completion, fulfillment—they all escape.

We Survive. But Not Always.
—Ralph

Jan's magical thinking was obviously dangerous. But magical thinking doesn't have to be, and it usually isn't.

My maternal grandfather, Otto Diebel (1884-1962), switched careers in the early 1900s for what many would consider magical, mystical reasons, according to my mother's telling. Desperate to help save his oldest daughter, Ruth, from succumbing to life-threatening illness (possibly influenza), he vowed to give his life over to God if she survived.

She did, so he did.

He had been delivering milk on the eastside of Detroit (before that he delivered beer, Pfeiffer's). But he became a priest in the New Apostolic Church and served until he retired in the 1950s.

One hundred years later, Otto's descendants are similarly wrestling with losses and limits, and what dealing with them means for the course of our lives. It isn't easy.

There was a time when I recoiled at the thought of life with a never-ending stutter, a lifelong limitation. How could I survive a life cursed with that? People would meet me and tell me later as an aside, "I didn't realize how terrible your stutter was," remarking on my endurance.

But guess what? It's no great feat. It's just my life.

My parents died four years apart when I was in my forties. During that first Christmas without either of them in 1998, I desperately wanted everything to be the way it was—when I was both the adored child and the munificent adult with my cherished young family. In that fleeting and rarefied midlife moment, I was a conduit for Christmases past, present and future. (It's hard to convey the exquisite perfection of this moment in the life of a family, although I've tried to signal that to my children, so they can luxuriate in it.)

The loss of my parents had left a crater in the family, and I ached with the strain of trying to make the family whole again.

Of course, the family was taking on a different shape even as I was going through the contortions required to maintain what was gone. In fact, I was taking an active role in what the family would become by fostering my own family with John.

Once again, this is how we survive: we refashion our lives to meet the new moment.

Research shows that people overestimate the degree to which undesirable events—losing a limb, developing diabetes, getting a colostomy, for example, or even living with face masks and social distancing—would negatively impact their quality of life.

"People are more resilient than they think they can be and can get through things that they probably would have never thought they could," concluded researcher Peter Ubel, M.D., one of my mentors when I was a U-M journalism fellow.

Now a physician and behavioral scientist at Duke University, Ubel was intrigued by why people generally imagine most illnesses to be much worse than people who actually have those illnesses report.

What he found was that people sync their lifegoals with the new limitations imposed on them by their illness, as he writes in his book, *You're Stronger Than You Think, Tapping into the Secrets of EmotionallyResilient People.*

I believe that, and at the same time I look at what happened to my sister and my brother, and I know viscerally that it doesn't always turn out that way. Sometimes magical thinking, or even resilience, just doesn't show up. And we can't conjure them, either.

In addition to circumstances, heredity/DNA plays a role in how much emotional resilience we have, but there's no clear understanding of how that works. Some researchers think DNA may influence happiness by as much as 50 percent, but it could be much less.

Life really is unfair, Ubel writes, and one of the primary reasons for that is DNA: "Some people are genetically inclined toward happiness, intelligence, optimism, and sociability, and others are not."

But—and this is a crucial qualifier—that leaves a significant opportunity for nongenetic factors to kick in and boost our resilience, including social, spiritual, intellectual and financial resources, he says.

Why they didn't in the case of my brother and sister remains a mystery to me.

While Jan's exit from the world was spectacularly mystical, my brother Ralph's was sadly common. At age fifty-eight, he died of cardiovascular and pulmonary disease exacerbated by alcohol abuse.

Ralph didn't want to leave us. He was depressed. He sought treatment several times, but finding the right medication is often a long and torturous process for those suffering from this illness. He self-medicated with alcohol and came to abuse it. And while he got sober several times, ultimately it didn't take. Meanwhile, he indulged in food and cigars with gusto. It is treacherous to be careless with your life.

Ralph was 363 days younger than me, and like all good younger siblings, regularly teased and tormented me. Throwing a lit firecracker into my cardboard Barbie Dream House was one of his more egregious acts, creating a hideous burn spot on the "carpet."

That, and trading our 45-RPM record of "I Want to Hold Your Hand" by the Beatles to one of his friends for five, count 'em five, other singles, including "Dominique" by The Singing Nun and "Hey, Paula," by Paul & Paula. The deal still makes me wince.

As we grew older, my sister and I gravitated toward college, my brother to a full-time job at the Ford Motor Company, where our father worked as a skilled tradesman, a millwright. Ralph became a tool-and-die maker and earned his journeyman's title, making a good life for his family.

I call his children, Angela and Keith, my "bonus kids" because they are mine in a way that transcends the usual connections of aunts and nieces and nephews. I have a fierce desire to hold them and the families they're creating close to me. I am the last remnant they have of their father. And for me they are living, thriving reminders of my brother's goodness.

He was also fun, and funny. In addition to his children, my brother loved his beagles. We had grown up with a beagle, Dandy (one of my dad's highest forms of praise was to call someone/something a "dandy," or "bub" in the case of his grandsons), and Ralph carried on the tradition with beagles of his own.

I took that and ran with it on his birthday in 1996. He shared the same name as country radio broadcaster Ralph Emery, who was credited with boosting the careers of many recording artists. I took a copy of

Emery siblings, me, Ralph and Jan, on Christmas Day. (1962)

his autobiography, *Memories*, and pasted my Ralph's photo on the cover, rewriting the author's note:

Over the course of 43 years, Ralph has launched the careers of enough great beagles to fill a veritable Beagle Hall of Fame, supporting them through good times and bad. In the 1950s, when other boys were yelping on the playground, Ralph Emery stubbornly continued to teach beagles to yelp, satisfying literally millions of grateful listeners. For four decades, Ralph has introduced the American public to performers such as Dandy I and Dandy II. Now, in Memories, he documents these years.

Born near the smelly mineral baths of Mount Clemens, Michigan, Ralph recalls the days of not only beagles but BB guns, firecrackers, and the most intriguing product of the time—salve. When he was only nine years old, Ralph and his family would gather around the mail-order cases and wonder aloud how he was going to unload all of that ointment for a Boy Scout fundraiser. Ralph had found his calling.

Yes, it was outrageously cheesy, but older sisters can be that way. I got the book when Ralph died.

It was in the early aughts, after our mother died and we became "orphans," that I noticed a growing change in Ralph. He started to joke about everything, in every conversation. He'd get across the information he had to relay, but it was surrounded by joking, which overtook more intimate conversation. It was as if he had to keep entertaining us, as if just being Ralph wasn't enough.

But we were rarely entertained. It was work just trying to endure, let alone respond to, the artifice he was erecting around his true self. That's the way I saw it, anyway.

I believe that's when his depression and drinking really took hold, contributing to the dissolution of his marriage and alternately scaring and alienating his kids.

Ralph relished hosting Thanksgiving dinner in the years after his divorce, although cooking was a skill he never really mastered. These were sometimes tense events, with Ralph either sober and trying too hard to please, or increasingly inebriated.

The day after Thanksgiving 2009 he sent me this message on Facebook, written in his trademark all-caps style and joking about the leftovers:

HEY SIS, I'VE GOT TURKEY SALAD, TURKEY SCAMPI, TURKEY SANDWICHES, TURKEY CASSEROLE, AND I THINK THAT'S IT.

Yes, "turkey scampi." The guy knew the lingo of fine cuisine, if not the actual meaning. His oven had been acting up on this particular Thanksgiving and the turkey never made it to being done. No one died, thankfully.

In the months before his death, Ralph was regularly

in and out of the hospital (high blood pressure, sleep apnea, etc.), contracting C. diff (Clostridium difficile), which didn't respond to treatment and meant he pretty much always had diarrhea. This did not help his depression.

Ralph's text messages to his daughter Angela reveal his descent:

9/22/11: Sober 10 days. Thinking of you. I love you.

11/20/11: Sick, tired + lonely. I need you more than ever, but I don't want to piss you off. I'll try harder, don't give up on me.

The last time I saw my brother, he finally wasn't joking. His son, Keith, and I sat with him at his kitchen table for what I guess you would call an intervention. (Angela had wisely opted to stay out of this conversation, as she had already raised his ire by regularly urging him to get help.)

We were tired and losing hope, and we were starting to feel powerless. No doubt he felt that way, too. We told him calmly but plainly that he was killing himself and that we were willing to do whatever it took to save him, but that we needed him to participate in the rescue.

Ralph said he knew that, but that his path "is what it is."

That place proved unreachable by us. So, we asked him if he wanted a funeral and how he wanted it to go.

I was surprised—he did want a send-off, and he laid out the basics for a memorial service and a luncheon.

Not long after, Angela called me crying, saying she was at her dad's and he wasn't answering the door. The police were on their way to break in.

Ralph was dead on the floor of his computer room. It was December 7, 2011, Pearl Harbor Day, now an infamous date in our own family history.

At his funeral, the young men in the Boy Scout troop Ralph helped lead spoke touchingly of his goodness. It was an important reminder. In the years preceding his death, when he was fighting the demons of depression and the lure of alcohol, his story became a nightmare for his children, his former wife, for me, and for those who knew him well.

The eulogies helped us remember the whole of his life, which was bigger than his disease.

A few months later we scattered his ashes in Buttermilk Creek at the family deer camp in northern Michigan near Manton, a place he loved. It was February, but the creek was still flowing.

Healing Dreams/Inner Voices

 Twenty months—Wresting the lead

I have been dancing with the behemoth that is memory.

At first it led with abandon, crushing my toes, my spirit, my will. Memory was stronger than my ability to go another way, to slacken the pace, to request another tune.

I let memory take me to that place that runs parallel with the world, where the wounded reside. There we lurch and sway with the unexpected direction memory takes us. We spin with the power of its lead. We lose ourselves in memory's embrace.

Until one day, we find footing on what seems to be another plane, another dance floor. We take a step, and memory follows *us*.

A whole new relationship begins.

Losing Jessica

There was no transition from life with Jessica to life without her. A few moments in time just blew up our existence. For a long time, I could barely hear my "just keep swimming" mantra, submerged as I was in undulating grief.

This is how she left us.

It was a warm, mid-August afternoon with roaring waves coming off Lake Huron and early dinner preparations under way. Jessica kissed me as she passed through the kitchen and said she was going down to swim with Caitlin and her friend Amalie. And that she loved me.

"OK, have fun. I love you, too." I was mixing the coleslaw. My response was rote, something I had tossed off a thousand times before.

Ten minutes later, I went down to watch the girls swim and saw that Jessica was not in the water with Caitlin and Amalie. My first thought was that she had gone to chat up our neighbors George and Carole, so I returned to the cottage and decided to give her a few minutes to come home before we had to go over and extract her. Jess loved holding court with a captive audience.

Another ten minutes passed and Caitlin and Amalie came up from the beach. I asked them to go get Jessica from George and Carole's.

The instant they came back with the news that she wasn't there, I knew from some deep, deep place within me that she was in trouble. What I hadn't even considered a moment before had suddenly become the only possibility.

I flew out of the cottage, John right behind me. Down the steps, to the path through the trees, onto the beach. My sandals filled with sand. I kicked them off so I could go faster. Pain shot through my bare feet as they slammed against the rocks and stones.

No matter, no matter. There she was, there, there. Face down in the water a bit farther down the beach. John moaned in agony, "Oh, my God, oh, my God."

"You need to help me," I said with words that were not yet a cry. At this point I believed I could still change the course of things. "You need to help me get her to shore."

Struggling against the rocks and waves, we pulled

Jess up onto the beach. A bluish tinge already tainted her face and lips. But maybe she had put on purple lipstick, her favorite color.

We had the presence of mind to try to empty Jess's lungs of water and then my husband started trying to blow life back into our daughter.

When he asked me frantically if we could indeed save her, I said yes, without hesitation. "Yes. Yes, we can." We had done this before—remember the delivery room? Remember how startled and amazed we were when she took her first breath, and we reveled in the power of having suddenly created a person? Remember making her first appointment with the pediatrician, giving a name to our creation and having her become part of real life? Remember that?

We can do it again. On this beach. Now. Right now.

George ran down from his house to help. The waves kept trying to reach Jess's face, like some taunting, unrelenting menace. I lay down and strad-dled her feet with my body, trying to keep the water away. I encouraged John and George—dear George, who had EMS training and probably realized it was too late but persisted with us anyway.

"Three more breaths, John, three more breaths," George kept saying after bearing down on Jess's chest to remind her heart that it was supposed to be beating. "Her color looks better than when we started, it looks better," George said.

While George and John were laboring to give Jessica a second birth, I was tugging at her one-piece bathing suit, trying to ensure that her private parts were covered. I had bought her a pair of swim shorts to help her deal with that, but she hadn't put them on.

Twenty minutes later, the ambulance crew sliced open the entire front of her suit to apply the defibrillator and jolt her back to life. The only electrical signal they got was the one going off from the vagus nerve stimulator in her chest, which was there to alert her to oncoming seizures. She had apparently seized as soon as she entered the water and went under the pounding waves.

The EMS workers said they would keep working on Jess en route to the hospital.

"OK," John and I responded without emotion, without even despair.

My mind went directly to how I could regain some control, exert some influence on this catastrophe. OK, I thought to myself, you guys keep working on that. And we'll make sure the insurance company knows Jess had to be taken to Cheboygan Memorial Hospital even though it might not be in-network for our insurance coverage ... "We couldn't choose where they took our drowned daughter, so if you're thinking of not covering this...." I was sure I'd have to convince them, so I was rehearsing what to say. I could do that. I could make that happen.

But no one was responding at the insurance company's 800 number.

At this point I think John and I were literally stunned—reduced to experiencing the world as just disembodied eyes and a whisper of breath. We did as were told; we followed the ambulance to the hospital.

But my husband and I were actually starting another journey. The moment the EMS workers took what was left of our firstborn, our dear Jessica, we miraculously headed in the other direction. Not bravely or confidently. Not even resolutely. We were shell-shocked, in no condition to determine our next moves beyond surviving the oncoming moment. But standing amid the onslaught of those moments were our three other children, and they needed to keep standing.

I don't know if I thought of this then or later, but there is a line from *Romeo and Juliet* where Romeo, referring to his friend Mercutio who has just been killed, says his soul "is but a little ways above our heads."

The sense that the deceased is somehow still with us in those initial moments of death is so compelling. And I believe Jessica's soul/spirit/energy was at work even then. It was watching out for John and me in the horror of her death, but especially for Caitlin and Amalie. It kept them at a safe remove from her body when they were coming up from the beach. It allowed Amalie to go tell our neighbor to call 911 when Caitlin was hysterical, distraught on the bathroom floor. It brought Amalie back to hold Caitlin's hand during this agony, as John and I tried to tend to the disaster overtaking our home.

And perhaps most amazingly, Jessica (in whatever form she had assumed at that moment) brought our dear friend Sarah—traveling to our cottage from Washington, D.C., an 800-mile sojourn—to our beach precisely when we needed her most. John and I were walking away from Jessica's body as it was being put into the ambulance, and suddenly Sarah was there.

You can call that happenstance, but in my version of this story the world is far too complex to assign such events to chance. So it was that John and I could follow the ambulance to the hospital, knowing Sarah, although gripped by grief herself, could comfort Caitlin and Amalie.

The truth is that early-stage grief is an agonizingly solitary experience. You have to let it penetrate painfully throughout your entire body before you can release it, ever so slowly, into the arms of someone else.

John and I didn't talk on the way to the hospital. We didn't cry, either. We just drove. Once there, we filled out forms and then waited . . . but no one came to tell us the obvious had been made official: that we could leave, without Jess.

We wanted to get out of there—that waiting room filled with tanned, weary-looking people in various stages of illness and pain that could all be fixed. They were alien to us. Losing Jess had catapulted us into an entirely new, unknown place. We wanted to go home to our family with the gaping wound. We wanted to find out if it would be fatal.

We told the receptionist we were leaving, and a frantic nurse came to stop us.

"I don't think you understand; your daughter is in a very critical situation," she said. It sounded like a scold.

We looked at each other and then at her. "She's dead, isn't she?" we asked.

Startled, she claimed that she didn't know but that we had to talk to a doctor. Soon another nurse asked us to step into a small examining room.

"I'm sorry, but we couldn't save your daughter. We worked on her as long as we could. But she's gone."

For all the tumult of the failed rescue, that's what it came down to. All the coming years of pain and loneliness turning on two words: she's gone.

We whimpered that we knew. The nurse handed me a Kleenex box and asked if we wanted some water. I did. I needed to take something from this person.

"I've been involved in resuscitating people who were near death," she said, "and they actually were mad when we were successful."

They had been peacefully on their way out and had resented being hauled back here.

We agreed that, yes, after the life-taking event itself, the transition to death was probably peaceful, as was the place Jessica was going. Wherever that was.

This is the question that would haunt me for months: Exactly where did Jessica go? I had lost a child, so of course I wanted to find her.

Later, perhaps comically, the Columbia University string-theory physicist Brian Greene became my guru. String theory insists that there are ten dimensions in space time, not just the four that we experience. Of course! She's there, just beyond reach in that parallel universe floating right next to ours, where multiple dimensions mingle in the "multiverse."

Caitlin, just fifteen but understanding the connections I was trying to make, told me about the uncertainty principle of quantum mechanics. You can't determine both the position and momentum of a particle; each has an inherent uncertainty. The universe is an uncertain place.

And so it is. For me, Jessica was just beyond the thin membrane of the world we knew. I decided it was too early to quit looking for her. I looked everywhere. Even in my dreams—especially in my dreams.

What does it mean to be dead? What does it mean as a physiological event, and what does it mean as a spiritual event? Finding the answers hurt. Like my feet pounding against the rocks to bring Jess up from the water. For months afterward, my feet ached when I got out of bed in the morning.

The nurse said she deeply regretted our loss but wondered if we'd consider donating Jessica's organs. She mentioned her eyes—those incredible blue eyes—and heart valves and bone tissue. Apparently

Jess had been dead too long to save the organs you always hear are in such short supply—heart, lungs, kidneys. So, I wondered, when did she die? Was it in the ambulance? Was it in the water? Was she indeed just a little ways above our heads on the beach?

I heard myself responding to the nurse, "Yes, whatever they need most."

Where did that come from? Was it during my fellowship at U-M, when I was studying life and death issues? Somehow, I had apparently reached a conclusion.

But wait. John and I hadn't discussed this yet. They were his organs, too. What did he want to do? He looked puzzled and pained.

"Are you sure," he asked me. "Are you really sure?"

"Yes. Yes, I'm positive." And so, he agreed.

Then they sent in the funeral home director—pulled away from his August-Saturday activities, no doubt—who said how very, very, very sorry he was. He seemed to want to hug us. We recoiled. The last thing we wanted was to hug our daughter's embalmer. So, he got more to the point: Did we want cremation or embalming?

John and I looked at each other. We knew we wanted cremation for ourselves, but this was different. I asked if we could think about it.

"OK, but not too long," he replied. They would have to start preparing pretty much right away if embalming was our choice.

Then John said, "Embalming, we want embalming."

I shrugged, OK.

The funeral home director said he would take care of everything and not to worry. Our daughter was in good hands. We resisted a good-bye hug.

The nurse asked if we wanted to see Jess before we left the hospital. We told her, almost in unison, that no, we didn't.

"She's not here anymore."

"No, she's not," the nurse replied in a voice that was barely there.

Healing Dreams/Inner Voices

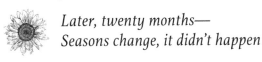 *Later, twenty months—*
Seasons change, it didn't happen

The change of seasons is so hard.

Especially spring. Friday was winter. And then on Saturday, creeping into Sunday, came that momentous transformation in the color and texture of the trees. There was a crack in the immutability of the way things are.

I dreamed that we had the wrong idea about Jessica dying. It turns out she had been damaged somehow in an accident but not killed. It was up to us if she would actually die. In the dream, Jessica didn't seem any different from the Jess we knew. I was elated. "It's okay. It's okay if she's damaged. We want her. We want her."

I woke up, and for the first time in twenty months, I was—if only for an instant—relieved and whole. For that moment, it didn't really happen.

The Family Impact
of Limits and Loss

I know those years when first Justin, then Ben, and eventually Caitlin were with Jess in the same school were hard: Jessica yelling wildly for their attention in the hallways; Jessica creating drama in common areas where she'd get the biggest audience, stomping her feet and hurling profanities. All of which they'd eventually hear about or be linked to by blood line. As if being a teenager wasn't hard enough.

We each had our own worst stories of Jess Attacks, including public meltdowns when it seemed like the whole world was watching and wondering what kind of family had produced this screeching, flailing human being.

It was a struggle to contain her outbursts as she grew bigger, even bigger than me. My moment of despair—maybe even a kind of disdain—came when she was in her late teens, in what I remember as The Bowling Alley Take-Down.

I had come to see Jess and her classmates bowl. And for one of those inexplicable reasons, the sight of me caused her such excitement/agitation that she knocked me to the floor. I remember seeing the ceiling swirling above me, along with the concerned heads that had gathered, and hearing screams and calls for security. I wondered: Am I still conscious or is this delirium?

Jessica's terrified shrieks startled me back to the unfolding scene. I was conscious; this was real life.

Justin has asked why we were so determined to integrate Jessica into the regular classroom, where her limitations and sometimes darn-right bizarre behavior were on full display.

Plain and simple: we were determined to make the world—starting with our local school—worthy of our children. All of them. The world met each of our other three children in a way we cherished; but it did not let in their sister, and that was simply not acceptable. I had defied diminished expectations for myself all my life. I wasn't going to let Jessica fall victim to them.

Separate is not equal, not only for Jessica but for other students who in the hoped-for future world would exist side-by-side with her, at work and in the community. A huge component in the education of children with disabilities is teaching them how to interact with others. Yet we spend no time teaching those without disabilities how to interact with people who have disabilities. As a result, they remain infuriatingly ignorant.

That is why we fought—and worked hard not to create any collateral damage. If we failed to protect our other children, my heart aches. But I believe we imparted important lessons about the value of human diversity. And maybe even lessons about living with loss and limits.

I cut out the guiding mantra for our parenting from a church bulletin. This was all I needed to know:

The

Family

Has a special vocation

To be a place

Where people are loved

Not for what they do

Or what they have

But simply

Because they are.

When she died, Jessica had just turned twenty-five and was about to enter her last year at Okemos High School. She would have to leave when she turned twenty-six, according to Michigan law. We weren't sure what she would graduate to, but we were ready to usher her into adulthood, including a life independent of us.

After you spend the early years of your disabled child's life defying cultural gravity, struggling to get her up the seemingly insurmountable precipice that will give her footing in the world, you have to get ready for the next phase: pushing her off.

For all the advances in neonatal care, early-childhood development and special education over the past half century—advances that our children with disabilities have not only enjoyed but in many cases owe their very existence to—we're still flummoxed by what to do with them once they grow out of the cute-kid phase. That makes parents' jobs twice as difficult. Not only do we have to prepare our child for a life in the world, but we also have to prepare the world for the life of our child. *That* is our colossal task.

The statistics illustrate the immensity of the challenge. Consider only the most basic social provisions we ask for our children: a job and a place to live.

About seventy percent of people with disabilities, many of whom want to work, are unemployed, according to the U.S. Bureau of Labor Statistics. That's outrageous and something we would never tolerate among able-bodied people. In this country, if you expect to receive social assistance, you have to work—even if you don't want to. But the vast majority of people with disabilities *want* to work. Society is the slacker when it comes to helping them do so.

Many adults with disabilities live with their parents until their parents are too old and frail to care for them; this crisis is now taking hold among the first people to grow up under special education laws, Jessica's generation. We have created an entire cadre of differently abled people, raised with the expectation that they would be one of us—that they would participate, contribute, thrive and grow. Despite new models for preparing students for jobs and providing housing alternatives, inclusion in community life eludes most people with disabilities.

This is the heartbreak that so clearly defines our job as parents, and early adulthood is when it comes into high relief. Our children need job skills, our children need social skills. But they also need a place to apply them, including a welcoming community. That means we have to work like hell to make a place for our children in the world.

One of the most powerful ways society reforms itself is when ordinary people see a conflict between what their children, or they themselves, are experiencing and what the world and its leaders are providing. For people with disabilities, the required experience is inclusion.

Do you want future citizens to be socially and morally responsible when "different" people move into their neighborhoods? Then you've got to expose them to people who aren't just like them.

This is uncomfortable for most people; this is hard. So be it. Until all children are fully included in the school community, no child receives a complete education. Until all people are allowed to work according to their ability, no social policy can succeed. And until all people are granted access to community life, no one lives a full life. In this, government plays a crucial role.

"To put something under the purview of government is to make a commitment to its essential importance," the writer and educator Nicholas Lemann has noted.

Yes! We were determinedly on that path, even as Jessica's challenges became more and more complicated. She developed intractable epilepsy as a teenager and over the years no medications stopped or even reduced the number of seizures she had. John kept an intricate daily diary of her medications and seizures.

Desperate, we spent a week at Henry Ford Hospital in Detroit, with Jessica hooked up with thirty-one electrodes, to see if the radical step of brain surgery might be an option. Doctors were trying to determine which part of her brain was responsible for the chemical misfires that caused her epilepsy. If the seizures were coming from an isolated place, that spot in her brain could possibly be removed and her seizures eradicated or at least lessened.

Jessica did not miss the opportunity to use her impending hospital stay to its best advantage; she

*Governor John Engler sent Jessica an encouraging
letter before she underwent a week of testing
at Henry Ford Hospital in Detroit to try to
stop her seizures. (2001)*

informed everyone she knew, and they responded. Even the governor.

Jessica would temporarily lose the ability to speak coherently following a seizure, so the doctors thought the seizure activity might have been centered in the part of her brain that controls speech. Speaking was one of Jessica's strong suits. People could almost look past her deficits once she started talking; in the right doses, she could be darn right engaging.

Were we willing to sacrifice those attributes—essentially much of the Jessica we knew—for a new, seizure-free Jessica? Could a misstep in fixing one problem create a whole new one? It would be a kind of Sophie's Choice.

The very notion of slicing and dicing my child seemed preposterous. But I also knew she needed to be freed from epilepsy's torment. All steps into the unknown are scary when you're taking your child with you. But most frightening of all are the options that tantalize you with hope.

John and I traded off staying at the hospital with Jessica in forty-eight-hour shifts, so one of us could be home with the other three kids. Exhausted, home for the night after my first shift, I heard Caitlin crying softly in her bedroom.

As if a trigger had been pulled, a recent dream came shooting back into my consciousness: I had had another baby, but I had forgotten to feed it!

I knocked on her bedroom door and pushed it open slowly. "What's wrong?" I asked, although what

I really wanted to say was, "Forgive me for screwing this up! How can I make it all—everything—right?"

But Caitlin wasn't accusatory, though I knew full well she could be. (Only a month earlier I stood charged with crippling her social growth by forbidding her to wear a strapless dress to the school dance.)

Instead, she seemed gripped by a wrenching emotional ache. I wanted the strapless-dress problem back.

I sat next to her on the bed. "I dreamed," she said slowly, "that they fixed Jessica and our whole family was on the *Today* show talking to Katie Couric."

I was stunned, and for the moment relieved. This did not seem like crying material to me. I figured I must be missing something. But how to avoid setting off an emotional avalanche with the wrong question? I responded cautiously. "And that wasn't a good thing?"

"No! It was awful," she sobbed, letting me hold her close, in a way that made me think I might actually be helping. "They fixed *everything*! Not just the seizures, but her learning disabilities—everything. It was a miracle, but she wasn't *our* Jessica anymore."

Exactly so. The pain of that realization made me feel as if I had been contemplating a sort of premeditated murder. Caitlin's sobs filled my ears and made my head throb, but I didn't let go of her.

We sat there trembling and sobbing, in celebration and regret, for all that we had and all that we didn't.

That might have been when we began to understand the power and the grace of being able to appreciate both.

Disability and illness should be honored as an important part of human diversity—they are facets of the limits to human perfection that illuminate our understanding of who we are and what the world around us is, and what it should be. They teach us about navigating adversity.

This role is not to be confused with "inspiration porn"—a term used by the late disability rights activist Stella Young for the portrayal of people with disabilities as inspiring others solely because they are disabled. She maintained in her TED Talk that able-bodied people put people with disabilities on a pedestal—find them "inspiring"—in part, because it makes them feel better about themselves, as in, "It could be worse. We could be disabled."

I follow my son Ben's friend Steve Gleason, who played six seasons with the New Orleans Saints, on Twitter. Steve famously blocked a punt in the first home game after Hurricane Katrina, and the play became a symbol of rebirth for the city. He has lived with ALS for more than ten years and is a leading advocate for people with the debilitating disease that has no cure. Steve is essentially immobile, although he can use his eyes to produce computer-generated speech.

Steve Gleason asked Ben to perform "Ends of the Earth" at the ceremony at the U.S. Capitol, when Steve was awarded the Congressional Gold Medal. (January 15, 2020)

You might call Steve inspirational, but I read him as instructive. One night he posted what seemed to be a revelation: "This is the greatest day of my life. I experienced the same challenges, and pain, but chose to receive them from a bigger/higher place."

Among the things that made his day so great? "I took Gray Gray [his daughter] to the lake. She is the most glorious creature."

That doesn't make me want to put Steve on high; it makes me want to apply that kind of thinking in my own life. It's practical advice.

Ultimately, we never had to make the decision about surgery for Jessica. The seizures were emanating from throughout her brain, so surgery wasn't an option. An alternative was to have a vagus nerve stimulator surgically inserted in her chest with a wire connecting it to the left vagus nerve, which would send signals to specific areas of her brain. Once activated, it was supposed to prevent seizures or at least let Jessica know when a seizure was coming so she could get to a safe place or simply sit down.

It didn't work out that way.

Healing Dreams/Inner Voices

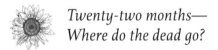 *Twenty-two months—*
Where do the dead go?

It's Sunday and Caitlin and I go to church. We look for a pew. I go in first.

There is Ardis Renkoski, a former neighbor whose daughter, Paige, has been missing for fourteen years. Her still-running car was found abandoned along I-96 with her shoes and purse still in it.

Fourteen years. I've been missing Jess for not quite two years. And I also have the consolation of knowing where she is. I helped put the headphones on her in the lavender casket right before they closed it.

Paige is presumed dead; no one really knows. But does Ardis presume? Does she believe amid evidence that is less than incontrovertible that her own flesh and blood is dead? Is Ardis in some child-less hell worse than mine?

Two wounds collide as Ardis and I try to find a comfort zone. We greet each other and exchange the usual niceties. But then Ardis gets right to the point: she is fine. The state attorney general may be interested in taking up Paige's cold case. There's a guy in prison who keeps taunting authorities. "I killed Paige," he says, "but you'll never get me on it."

In that instant I want to kill him, even though I know he must be the son of another effectively child-less mother who somehow lost her boy along the way. Death isn't the only way to lose a child. They can disappear, they can grow up badly.

I am deep into that thought when the mass starts. Ardis and I pray together. We sing together. And in what must have been our spiritual destiny for that day, we offer each other the only salve we know:

"Peace be with you."

We embrace to seal the deal.

Losing Jessica, cont.

After leaving the body that was Jess at the hospital, John and I drove back to the cottage, but I don't remember that. We were desperate to leave the lake. We had driven to the cottage in two cars, so we wanted to get both of them back home. Who knew what fortifications might be needed in the coming days? Two cars might be important.

But that meant driving the four hours home in separate cars. John, alone in the station wagon, me with Caitlin and Amalie in the Cutlass. I kept reassuring myself that we could do this. We could. Do this.

We started to gather up our things. Sarah asked if she could help, and I indicated that we were beyond help. It's a statement I ultimately regretted, for it cast Sarah into the same desperate place as we were. I had also sent the neighbors George and Carole away. Later I would come to understand this as one of the lowest points of my despair, when I was utterly incapable of accepting assistance, defiant of my place among the bereft. When you can't accept help, when you cannot acknowledge the gift of helpers, you are unlikely to ever find your way back to gratitude, which is where happiness begins.

Deep within grieving, giving thanks is impossible. You are overcome by sadness, loneliness, loss. There is nothing to be grateful for. Then comes the moment when you realize that your friends are trying to help you. Having emerged from your grief just long enough to catch a fleeting glimpse, it comes as a revelation: you are thankful for them. That is the beginning of finding your way out.

I grabbed a trash bag and threw in as many of Jessica's things as I could. I told Sarah I wanted to spare John the excruciating pain of seeing them again, so I was taking Jess's things away. As if there were such a place to stash pain. How far away would that have to be? I started imagining that John would fall apart. That without Jessica he would cease to be the man who was Jessica's father.

John had similar fears. We were desperate to retain any scrap of what we had.

"We have to get through this," he insisted when we arrived home that night. "We can't let this break up our family."

And yet my husband was the mirror image of my pain. And the last thing I wanted was twice of what was already threatening to consume me.

I stuffed the bag with all of Jessica's things—the papers, the pencils, Harry Potter books, including page upon page of the same photocopied picture of Harry—into the far reaches of my car trunk. And I made sure it was me who retrieved the bag when we got home. Of course, I could no more protect John from this excruciating pain than I could protect myself from it. But I didn't know that then.

I was desperate to leave the cottage and decided to head out first. John wanted me to wait, but perhaps sensing my need to flee, he said he would be right behind me. I turned on National Public Radio and waited for the sounds of crying from Caitlin and Amalie in the back seat. But there were none; just silence. Silence I could bear.

I kept expecting to see John in my rearview mirror. I had started out going just over the speed limit, so as to get home quicker. Then I realized that I didn't really want to get home as much as I wanted to see my husband. I slowed down and regretted that I had left without him.

Forty-five minutes passed and I began to think about that unspoken wish among the parents of disabled children: that our children should die five minutes before we do.

That may sound macabre unless you've been haunted by fears of what an indifferent world—it wouldn't even have to be cruel—could do to your vulnerable child. Who would take care of her, who would protect her, how would she live? At least after your child dies, you know she is safe from the dangers of this world.

I started to worry that something had happened to John. Maybe in his grief he hadn't been watching the road and ... I decelerated further, to the minimum speed limit. (Ever wonder who those people going fifty-five in the right lane of the expressway are? They are the wounded; they are the just-surviving. And in your rearview mirror, they do indeed look farther away than they really are.)

I remembered John saying a couple hours before, as we waited at the hospital, "Well, I've lived fifty-three good years," as if there were an allotment on happiness and that once the unbearable had happened, it was all over. What is the life span of happiness? Had we already enjoyed our share?

I fixated on my rearview mirror and had to remind myself to watch the road ahead. I started thinking this might be a metaphor for my future—so consumed by the past that I'd ignore what was coming. Where was he?

As darkness fell, I realized that he was in *front* of me. I had somehow missed seeing him go by. I settled a bit more comfortably into the driver's seat.

A couple of hours into the trip when we had driven out of NPR range, a Top-40 station came on the radio. I heard some talking and gentle laughter coming from the back seat and marveled at how that could be. A part of me resented it, even. How could Caitlin and Amalie not be distraught beyond words, let alone beyond laughter? Maybe they had already found a way out of this oppressive gloom—not an escape but a way to survive.

We dropped off Amalie at her father's house. He offered to help in any way he could and hugged me in the sympathetic blackness of the night. Then he went into his house with his daughter. The simple exquisiteness of that event brought me to tears.

Providing a home, a safe haven, is so integral to being a parent. And because Jessica had disabilities, it became something of a sacred mission for John and me. Jessica reveled in being at home, in her purple bedroom, on her violet sheets, surrounded by the photos that brought her so much comfort. Her room seemed to ache with her loss.

Resisting the anticipation of her arrival home at the usual times was one of the bitterest adjustments we had to make. We kept waiting for her to walk in.

The problem with the dead is not that they're gone, it's that they never come home. The heartbreak is in the yearning.

For months I feared seeing school buses in the late afternoon, taking their charges home, Jessica nowhere to be seen. They drove right through the gaping hole in my heart.

Healing Dreams/Inner Voices

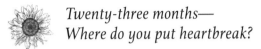 *Twenty-three months—*
Where do you put heartbreak?

Jessica's friend Tim returned her Rock & Roll Hall of Fame pen and a photo of her that I had given him as a remembrance.

He said they made him too sad.

I know what he means.

I reread the note he sent us soon after Jess died:

Jessica she was a hero.

She was always friendly and made me feel happy.

She died in the water.

We were in love.

Boyfriend and girlfriend.

Good-bye.

I wanted to exchange this heartbreak for something else, but I knew it would always be mine.

A Breaking Home

From the cottage John and I drove directly to our house, where our unsuspecting son Justin was watching a movie with friends. John whispered to him that something had happened, and it would be better if his friends left. (Nineteen-year-old Ben was traveling in Canada; we hadn't been able to reach him yet.)

John told Justin the incomprehensible news before Caitlin and I arrived home, and I remember the horror in his face as I walked through the door. Dear Justin, the eldest by default, although Jessica was more than two years older. Finishing up his senior year at Michigan State University, preparing for a career in journalism. I wanted to absorb all the pain and hurt in his eyes and tried to fortify myself to do that.

The four of us collided in our grief: all grasping arms, crying eyes, wailing voices in a tight huddle. That's all there was for what seemed like a very long time. Staring at each other in disbelief, desperately trying to resist the reality that someone so intimately connected to our lives, to life as we knew it, was forever gone. Disappeared.

For weeks after, we stumbled through the warp that is new grief. Time doesn't really exist there. You can rouse memories, but the progression of time is missing, even though the clock moves on. Grief is the void; you are there with your heightened senses only—all-feeling, exposed and dangerously vulnerable.

Gift of Life called close to midnight. I answered a laundry list of questions so they could determine the probable condition of Jessica's donated tissue. What they were trying to get at was whether Jess was a drug abuser or sexually promiscuous. So, some of the questions had to do with her behavior. They warned me that these questions were coming and could be painful.

But what struck me was how circumscribed her life had been. She was about as pristine as they come, something John and I worried about as she grew out of our household. People with intellectual disabilities are sexually assaulted at rates more than seven times those of people without disabilities, according to U.S. Justice Department statistics reported by

National Public Radio. That is one of the highest rates of sexual assault of any group, but it's rarely talked about.

I agonized over her first gynecological exam, searching for a woman doctor to stress the point that such a probing of her body was to be done only in a doctor's office and certainly not by a man. Of course, abusers could be women, too, and such intimacy could actually be appropriate, as with a lover. But I couldn't set up a system that would accommodate those exceptions; a blanket ban was all the protection I could offer.

On the phone with Gift of Life, I was able to give away her beautiful blue eyes but not her forearms, which someone apparently needed for the bone tissue. No, I wanted those in the casket with her, adorned with the blue bracelet we had given to her for her twenty-fifth birthday six weeks before.

I knew the moment I gave away Jessica's eyes and skin that those were the very parts of her that I would miss the most. Her eyes, those windows to the soul, so blue that people often remarked about them. Her great aunt said they were evidence that there was something special about her—as if we needed any proof. Her skin, its texture and smell, conjured such vivid memories that I'd be momentarily startled to find a full-grown woman in my arms when we hugged, rather than the child I was imagining.

Still, in the earliest moments of making my way through the buffered existence that is grief, answering

You were a gift
from the very beginning.

Jessica Emery Schneider
Donor

*Jessica was among the organ donors honored at a Gift of Life
ceremony at the Michigan Capitol in Lansing. (2011)*

"yes" to the question of whether we wanted to donate Jessica's organs was one of the surest things we did.

That was when the next phase of guiding our child through life—the entire cycle of life, including death—began. Miraculously, her eyes, bones and heart valves—no longer of use to her—could improve life and possibly even create additional days for other people. We didn't succeed in saving her for ourselves on that warm August afternoon, but her gifts would now extend beyond our dreams.

That first night we all slept—or at least lay down—in the same room. John and I in our bed, and Caitlin and Justin in sleeping bags on the floor nearby. Amid a darkness that seemed to be within us, as well as all around us, we wanted to establish a bulwark so that not one of us would be swept away by grief. We'd all be there to pull the others back. To be pulled back ourselves.

It seemed I could take only constricted, shallow breaths. I was fearful of breathing deeply, as if having that much of my life inside me would be too much to bear. If sleep overtook me, it was quickly doused by tears, startling me into the torture of consciousness. Jessica's death was everywhere. In the darkness, my entire being was reduced to my beating, aching heart.

We couldn't reach Ben for two days. The number he had given us only took messages that he never received.

Waiting, yearning for and yet dreading the moment we'd finally reach him, we agonized over what to tell him. It would take perhaps five hours for him to drive home. Would he become so distraught with the news that he would be unable to stay focused on driving safely? But if we didn't tell him, how would we explain the need for him to come home immediately? Would he imagine a horror even worse than the one that awaited him?

The vulnerability of each of my children began to terrify me. Forty-six days after Jessica died, I dreamed Caitlin was among several children floating face-down in some nondescript body of water. The thought that I was destined to lose all my children this way shrieked through my dreaming brain, and I frantically started turning over the bodies. I woke up to realize Caitlin was safely asleep in her bed. And Jessica was already dead.

Ben finally returned home, and we told him the unfathomable—Jessica was no longer here. He processed it by wailing alone in his room, often shrieking, and not softly. We asked through the closed door if he needed anything. He said he didn't, but we worried. Jess was gone, but we were still here.

Six hours later, he emerged with a painting of a laughing Jessica. We cried and hung it on her bedroom wall.

Surviving the death of a child makes you hypervigilant about ensuring the survival of your remaining children. Justin and Ben were in college, so I worried about how they would absorb the impact of losing Jess and how I would know if they were prevailing

Ben's portrait of Jessica.

against the pain. Caitlin, still in high school, would be with John and me. In concept, I assured myself, we would be able to confirm her status every day.

But amid the emotional chaos, Justin, Ben, and Caitlin did a remarkable thing: the day before Jessica's funeral, on August 20, 2002, they went to a photo booth and posed for four photos, making all the goofy faces photo booths inspire. And then they gave it to me.

I was initially stunned and confused. Why were they being so silly at this moment of utter despair? And why were they dragging me into it, flaunting their ability to rise above the abyss that was threatening to engulf me?

But that, I ultimately determined, was exactly what they were trying to tell me: They *would* survive.

Of course, this was just the beginning of their journeys through grief. I knew they couldn't get to the other side without experiencing the pain that loss extracts. John and I could only fretfully watch ... and catch them if they lost their footing.

Five years later, when they were all home for Christmas 2007, the three of them posed for another photo booth shot. For me these photos were "proof of life," a phrase used to describe evidence that a kidnap victim is still alive. My remaining children *were* surviving.

Justin, Ben and Caitlin posing in a photo booth right after Jess died in 2002, and again five years later.

Healing Dreams/Inner Voices

 Two Years—When memory steals your breath

When I'm remembering Jess, it can still literally take my breath away.

Her memory comes rushing in. And I have to physically struggle to inhale the air that no longer animates my Jessica.

It feels like a kind of suffocation.

Struggling to Survive

Before the survival of our remaining children could become clear, we had to see Jessica (and ourselves) through the final phase of her worldly existence.

The rote requirements of dealing with death—the ritual of it all—had to be addressed: the funeral, the viewing, the burial, the casket (lavender), her clothes (a new bra and purple sweater picked out by Caitlin, me, Jessica's Aunt Mary and cousin Ellie.)

We would deal with surviving without her later... and forever.

I wrote the eulogy for Father Mark to give at Jessica's funeral at St. John Student Parish in East Lansing. (Yes, I made him get on my soapbox....)

As parents and as a society, it is our job to make the world worthy of our children. Above all else, that is our mission.

But the fact is that the world is often not worthy of our children, and it is certainly not worthy of our disabled children.

While great gains were made in special education during Jessica's lifetime, after finishing school disabled people often face a bleak world. Unemployment among disabled people is at seventy percent, most do not live independently.

Jessica touched all of you here in some way. She taught you something about tolerance, something about acceptance. She had an amazing ability to do at least that one thing spectacularly well.

Having received that from her, you here are all charged by her death to go out into the world and perform at least one act that will improve the lives of the disabled.

If you are an employer, you need to hire a disabled person.

If you are an employee or a customer, you need to be more patient with a disabled worker.

If you are a voter and there's a bus millage on the ballot that will permit the disabled to get to work, you need to vote for it.

If you are a student, you need to go the extra mile

for a disabled classmate, even though they may embarrass you.

Jessica changed us all; now we are called to take up the charge inspired by her life.

After the funeral we started living two parallel lives: the real life, where we were at home together with our grief and memories, and the pretend life, where we worked and shopped and did what we had to do to survive.

At some point, perhaps, these two existences would merge. But I couldn't imagine when that would be. Life outside our grief was no longer our real life. It was what we did meanwhile ... What was real was the emptiness.

Without consciously thinking about it, I began honoring ritual. Scores of flower arrangements had been sent to the funeral home. When they called asking what they should do with them, I said I wanted them—all of them. Over the next week, John and I took them all to Jessica's grave, in a regular procession, half a mile down Dobie Road, to Leek Cemetery.

In another part of the ritual, I began reliving the hours of each day according to how they unfolded on the day she died. Remembering especially the dread of 3 p.m. to 4 p.m., when she went from life to death.

In Jessica's death notice we requested contributions to the Okemos Special Needs Day Camp where, as we explained, she had spent "many a glorious summer." I began tracking how far those gifts would take the remaining kids at the camp. In addition, we eventually saved enough money and held enough fundraisers to establish an endowment at the MSU Community Music School, the Jessica Emery Schneider Music Therapy Services Fund.

Music was one of the most important salves of Jessica's short life, and the endowment was set up to fund technology that allows people without the motor skills to play instruments to still make music. Some of Jessica's friends benefit as participants in the school's annual Eric "RicStar" Winter Music Therapy Camp, a program started by our friends Dick and Judy Winter in honor of their late son, Eric, who also had a disability. We wanted to make sure Jess's life had made a difference in the world; that the world was changed for her having been in it.

The "Servant Song," by Richard Gillard, in the church hymnal had always resonated with me, so we asked the St. John Student Parish choir to sing it at Jessica's funeral. We are all pilgrims on a journey, the lyrics say, and our purpose is to help each other "walk the mile and bear the load."

But now other verses drew me in—the ones noting that while we should serve one another, there was also grace in being served, in accepting help.

At that moment, that is what I needed to learn.

I was always the helper, and I liked it that way. But the experience of emotional devastation is so life-shattering that you simply cannot reconstruct the pieces without the warm hands of friends and family to help meld them again.

These people, your tribe, often know where the pieces go when you, in your grief, do not. Be open to what they are offering. Take their help. Eventually, perhaps even exquisitely, the shattered pieces can develop a beauty all their own in the repaired piece that is your life.

Two weeks after Jess died, John insisted that we return to the cottage. We had to confront the place that had swallowed up our daughter. The idea made me physically sick, and I resisted the plan. But he was adamant that we not allow the place that had been our sacred refuge to instead become our tormentor. So we went.

Embracing what you fear is so difficult. But to get to comfort you must endure discomfort—you must seek it out, go there, enter in, risk the experience.

I could hardly breathe as we approached the cottage. And I became sick to my stomach as we settled in.

But eventually it subsided. And we noticed something yellow—a toy?—down on the beach. I pulled out the binoculars.

It was a sunflower growing among the rocks and sand! How had a sunflower seed ended up there? What had nourished it? How had it survived growing so close to Lake Huron's pounding waves? How did it happen to be in full bloom at this moment?

The improbable sunflower.

The joy of stumbling upon a spectacular find gave way to the notion that this was a sign. A sign from Jess, on the beach where she died: The sunflower was blooming just for us. We hadn't brought a camera—this was before cell phones—so I drove to Kmart for a disposable camera and used up a roll of film taking pictures of the sunflower. I knew this was our Christmas card.

This, too, became part of my rituals. Our cards read:

As the star was for the three wise men, so this sunflower—growing improbably in the sand and rocks on our beach just two weeks after Jessica's death—has been an inspiration for us. May you know the blessings of proceeding in hope this Christmas season and beyond.

I rejected the wording proceeding *with* hope. The hope couldn't be a distinct thing that you might not remember to bring with you. It had to be bigger than that. It had to be an aura, an atmosphere. Something you were in no danger of losing: proceeding *in* hope.

John's Christmas gift to me that year was a painting of the sunflower, created by a local artist who had painted it from one of my sunflower photos.

The last time I was down on our beach that year, just after Christmas, all that remained of the sunflower was six inches of broken-off stem. It was brown and brittle, tenuously holding its own against the building ice and snow. I knew the feeling.

Healing Dreams/Inner Voices

 Twenty-seven months—Finding gratitude

I am home alone today but not really alone.

Jessica's cat follows me from room to room. Right now, she's sitting in the sunlight streaming through the window as I work at the computer.

I am reminded of how Jess loved to do that, loved to just *be* with you—her family and friends, but really anyone who took the time to greet and engage her. What a gift she had, always to be with you in the moment.

Incredibly, I'm starting to feel grateful for the whole of it: Jessica's birth, her life ... even her death. Which is so hard to say. But with the wide lens that gratefulness provides, I can see each distinct phase of her existence so clearly, from birth right up until the end. And I can also see the inextricable linkage of those phases: each exists because of the others, even the ending.

They are all a part of what was Jessica, my daughter.

The Aftermath

Early on, living with the reality of Jessica's death involved a dual process of both succumbing to grief and resisting it. Great loss is immutable; it just is, so you accommodate it however you can.

Initially, mired in a stunned existence, you ride the ebb and flow of survival and despair, hanging on for dear life. Gradually, over time, you discover where the loss fits in your life. This is the key to everything—*every thing*. This is what life is all about: learning to live with the losses that come your way.

There is no clear way out because, in fact, you can never get out; those losses become part of who you are. So, your crucible is to mold a life that includes that negative space. You must find a place for it so you can continue the journey.

Twenty-five days after Jess died, on the first anniversary of the 9/11 terrorist attacks, I tried to write something that might merge my single, solitary loss—the one threatening to overwhelm me—with the grief of all those thousands of people who had lost family in the terrorist attacks.

All I could manage was three short sentences. Not quite the essay I had envisioned but, perhaps, a poem:

> *The human heart*
> *longs to know*
> *The trajectory*
> *of the grief it must bear.*
> *It wants to know*
> *how long it will last.*
> *How deep it will go.*
> *And,*
> *most of all,*
> *when it will end.*

I wondered if maybe it wasn't my time to be contributing anything. Maybe it was my time to be taking. I always wanted to be the consoler, the giver, the provider, so this was difficult for me.

The ceremonies honoring the first 9/11 anniversary provided the solace I needed. I was looking for comfort, I was looking to learn something. I figured that the victims of 9/11 who were not killed that day had now lived with the abyss for 365 days. Long enough to experience all the annual reminders of loss that I was dreading—birthdays, anniversaries, holidays.

Having grudgingly given over one year to despair,

the salve of time had perhaps granted grievers the tantalizing prospect that at some distant time, their grief and joy might coexist. The grief would always be there, but there would be room for something else. That hope might not be full-blown at one year, but it might at least be perceptible. Or so I prayed.

John and I had entered the wounded legion of "child-less" (not necessarily without children, but without a certain child) parents. Our first-born was permanently missing from the world, so there was less of us here, too. Us, less Jessica. Preposterous.

We heard from many "child-less" parents. They sought us out. They told us touching stories of their grief. One woman said it seemed like just yesterday since she had lost her six-year-old in a choking accident, and she recounted the incident in great detail.

It was forty-six years ago.

Still, I was beginning to emerge from that early period when the pain of losing Jessica startled me upon waking and immediately sucked me into its vortex. Her death had become a huge hole that no longer consumed me but still took up nearly all aspects of my day. I'd carve out small spaces for work, and for the activities vital to everyday life, but the hole was always threatening to overtake them.

People told me that at some point the hole would shrink so that I could actually put it away, to sometimes forget about it. But not now. On September 11, 2002, I was thankful merely for the ability to cry for someone else.

John wrote regular installments about our life after Jessica's death in his Sunday columns for the *Lansing State Journal*. The pieces were beautifully and sensitively written, recounting the simple things he missed—listening to Detroit Tigers baseball games on the radio with her, the loss of which readers mourned with him.

Most poignantly, he wrote about fishing with Jess at sunrise, when the rest of the family wouldn't budge from our beds at the cottage. How the gentle rocking of the boat soothed her, how he recorded her presence in the boat log every time they caught a big one.

Jess lovingly called my husband a "fishing fanatic." And Scottish politician John Buchan's description of the sport confirmed for me that John's affinity was a noble cause: "The charm of fishing is the pursuit of what is elusive but attainable, a perpetual series of occasions for hope."

That was the pursuit we were on with Jess—during her lifetime and after, in living without her. Fishing was as good a place as any to learn the resolve hope requires.

I began thinking of John's columns as an exquisite butterfly collection, the delicate "wings" of our grief pinned in a display box. Looking at it, it seemed the butterflies had no bodies because that part of them was so small, and the wings were such a distraction. But there *were* bodies—the butterflies were dead.

I tried to imagine what I would write about. How would I convey that what I missed so desperately was

John and Jess celebrate their catch.

her smell? And who would understand that? We gave away most of her clothes soon after Jess died, but the scent of the shirts we kept revived her in my memory. How could it be that my daughter existed only as memory?

I missed her skin. Soft, warm, fleshy. Jessica wasn't overweight, but she had low muscle tone. Maybe that's why my lips seemed to sink into her skin during "cozy time," which we invented when the kids were small. I'd come in and lie with them just before they fell asleep.

The three younger kids outgrew the ritual but not Jess. Even in the weeks just before her death, I'd lie with her—she sometimes cradled me—as the TV screen flickered the tape of some long-ago TV show she loved, or an old rerun of the news. She loved the news. It didn't have to be new news. She loved seeing the same people, predictably and reassuringly recounting the day's events.

When I went to bed one night soon after her death, I laid with a bent arm over my eyes. I rotated my arm slightly inward and realized that when it brushed across my lips, the inside of my forearm was the same texture as Jessica's face. I began kissing it furtively, and thanked the darkness for its cover. How weird is this, I wondered, as my mouth gave way to sobs.

The thing about children dying is that they are in more danger of disappearing than people who die older, with more accomplishments and relationships to connect them to the world. So, one Saturday in October, Jessica's headstone suddenly became an urgent concern. I started panicking that we had waited too long, that they wouldn't be able to erect it by winter and that we wouldn't be able to find her grave beneath the snow. Then we would *really* have lost her.

We spent the weekend picking out a headstone for Jess and writing our own epitaph. Our names would be on the stone, too. Some people are appalled by the idea of putting their own name on a tombstone, but that's exactly what I wanted to do. I didn't want to leave her in the cemetery alone.

I agonized over the stone, the engraving, the wording. But in the end, there was no question what our lives came down to. We had held up our corner of the world by firmly grasping hands and refusing to let go.

A note from Cathy, an office worker at the high school who befriended and loved Jess, confirmed it:

"I think of Jess often and her comments about 'Know what my sister put in my lunch? A cookie, wasn't that nice, Cathy?' Or, 'My brother waved at me in the hallway!' Or, 'I saw my dad kiss my mom!' You all made her so happy!"

If the key to human happiness is the consciousness of being beloved, as Adam Smith maintained, then we had had it all. Ultimately, as her headstone noted, we were:

Grateful to God.
Honored to have loved each other
and our children, Jessica, Justin, Benjamin and Caitlin

On our ninety-sixth day without Jess, the cemetery sexton called to say that the monument had been put in place. It was windy, drizzling, cold and dark when I got home from work, but we didn't want to wait until morning to see it. We took a flashlight and found the gray monument that honored the place where Jess was buried.

From now on, this would be the sign of Jessica's presence in the world. The hugs, the smiles and the ebullient greetings that had once been her gifts were gone, but this place would trigger memories of them. And in one hundred years, when no one remembered her, someone walking by would stop and say, "Look, Jessica was just twenty-five. Her parents had to bury her."

Our light found the stone and then the words: SCHNEIDER, Jessica E. 1977-2002. It was shocking, but our names engraved next to hers seemed right. That's where we should be: Sharon Emery, 1952—, John B., 1949—. She wasn't alone; we were right there.

John and I cried and hugged each other, ignoring— or maybe, defying—the wind and rain that battered us.

"We did it right," he said. "It looks good."

We started the ritual of putting purple-painted

stones atop the monument each time we visited. We kept a pail of the stones there so we would know if others had come to keep Jess company. And they did; they still do.

The cemetery became a community to me, going there a kind of social event. As I'd walk up the drive into Jessica's section, I'd imagine her being with the two other young women buried close by: Janelle, nineteen, and Amanda, twenty. If no one was around, and usually nobody was, I'd greet them out loud. I'd ask them how things were going and tell them how I was. Sometimes I'd even articulate Jessica's answers in her characteristic phrasing. She was fine. She was glad to see me.

I made sure to say Jessica's name aloud at least once a day, so I could revel in remembering a time when that word had a destination, a purpose—when it belonged to something alive and beautiful and thriving in the world. Saying her name was necessary to establish her existence for her first doctor's appointment; now it was necessary to say it to confirm that she still existed in my new, expanded world.

Such rituals helped me survive, connecting me to some larger realm where everything we've lost resides. All the important things we need to learn are there. So even though we may not want to, we have to go there to figure out what the losses mean, to make sense of them. There must be lessons in the losses. They must be significant.

I said this, but I didn't yet believe it.

The role of bereaved parent confers a special status on the bearer—that of The Tragically Wounded—reflecting what the world sees as a frightening and remote state of being. ("I can't imagine what you're going through.") So often, people don't know what to say to the profoundly grief-stricken.

What they should know is that they cannot diminish or increase my grief, which exists totally apart from their influence. They are simply not that powerful. What they *can* provide is a safe place for The Grieving to find another facet of their pain, so it doesn't remain a sheer cliff that bottoms out in desperation.

How do The Grieving find this place? The Temporarily Non-Grieving listen—simply listen—to them. Their power is in receiving what is being said, in allowing The Grieving to define their shapeless, all-encompassing pain so they can make footholds that keep them above the abyss.

That said, there is an aspect to grief that is necessarily a solitary journey. What I seek, but what scares me in its other-worldliness, is the presence of Jessica and my mother, who died three years before Jess. And that of my sister, Jan. I can find them at night, if I really concentrate—pray, meditate, whatever you want to call it. If I really *listen*.

The comforting hugs and kisses and gentle stroking from my dear friends and family are necessarily external. Jessica and my mother give me comfort that emanates from within me. It starts out weak, as a faint heat and fullness in my chest. Then it grows until my whole body is overflowing with their presence. And I cry softly with joy.

There is a deeper intelligence that comes from pausing/contemplating/taking time, and because the depths of human experience are more than physical, you should look for those opportunities. It's like a sense you didn't realize you had.

I'm fascinated by the concept of the multiverse— that hypothetical collection of innumerable universes including our own, some with totally different physics and numbers of spatial dimensions, where all of us and everything else exists in countless copies—because that means Jess still exists somewhere. The everlasting life that religions around the world profess may exist in a realm we can barely contemplate at this point in human evolution. They say that people see angels in that space where mystical/spiritual beliefs seep into their experience of real life. I have seen these angels.

When I experience that extra sense, Jessica is within me as she was in the earliest days of her existence, those nine months when she grew from a hope in my heart to a living, breathing, wild-haired newborn. The bond with a child begins long before the moment of birth.

But it also exists long after the moment of death. A grieving mother just plays out the birthing process in reverse. Those moments when I feel her presence now are merely part of the same circle of her life that I experienced when she was newly growing within me. She has moved on, but we are eternally connected.

Sometimes I lose faith in the power to make the connection, and with it the conduit to Jessica. Two months after her death, I was still trying to figure out where Jess went. We "lost" Jessica, as the euphemism goes. So, if Jessica was lost to us, then like all parents of missing children, we were desperately searching for her. Even in death.

Were there answers I just wasn't seeing? How does God speak? Via nature? In the transfiguration of the leaves in autumn? That beauty seemed audacious in the face of my grief. In the random, improbable blooming of a sunflower? Give me a break. That's too precious, a cliché.

On Day Seventy-One without her, I just wanted Jess back.

I set upon making a homecoming dance dress for Caitlin. Voila—a perfect distraction for my grief. One that even produced results. The black-and-white ensemble went together with barely a tantrum on my part, and it fit perfectly. Even more amazing, Caitlin liked it.

We took photos, and as I walked around Target while they were being processed, I had a growing dread. The pictures of Caitlin in her grown-up finery were at the end of a roll of film that included the last photos taken of Jessica, posing with John and my brother, Ralph, with their all-time record catch: a twenty-six-pound salmon.

It was a perfect metaphor for the way our grief resides with our joy, each diluting the other in a new mix that makes them both more precious. I started thinking more and more about my journalism fellowship studies and how the value of limits—on happiness, on all things good—plays into life.

I had never really questioned why we had a child with disabilities. In fact, I remember being with Jess, Justin and Ben in our sweltering house in Lansing during the particularly hot summer of 1983, soon after Ben was born. There was an Ethiopian mother on the news who was starving to death along with her children in the worst famine to hit the country in a century.

I marveled at why that wasn't me and my children. What miracle had instead placed me in Lansing, Michigan, in a frame colonial with three bedrooms, a stocked refrigerator and a "disabled" daughter, unscathed by famine?

My good fortune was plain to see, and I knew it required something from me in return. My job— among all those the world needed done—was to ensure that the great value of our disabled daughter, my children's sister, and others like her was recognized and appreciated. The public, and even teachers and doctors, underestimate the quality of the lives lived by disabled people. "Quality of life" is far too individualized an experience to be predicated on abilities. By that definition, "talented" people—those exceeding at the activities that society currently extols: athletes, actors, inventors—would all be happy.

People of advanced age and those with disabilities are a presence to be valued because they show us the diversity of human experience which, if we survive long enough, we all will come to exemplify. In short, we need to make the world worthy of "them," who ultimately will be "us."

That's not to say it's easy. There's a tendency to remember only the good times and, therefore, idealize Jessica in a way that is not honest or true. In mid-November 2002, Caitlin and I spent five-and-a-half hours at the Detroit Institute of Arts. We saw an Edgar Degas exhibit in a crowded museum, then had lunch and finally coffee in a busy café. We could never have done that with Jess, who would have been disruptive and loud, impatient and frustrated.

We met Jessica's Aunt Mary and cousin Anna for breakfast at Detroit's Eastern Market the next day. We spent an hour looking for knickknacks in a crowded warehouse shop. I didn't have to worry that Jess might break something. Or have a seizure and fall into a display. Or freak out in the crush of shoppers.

The cold wind blew through the open stalls of produce. The holiday grave blankets were piled high. Some had purple ribbons. I was not yet ready to buy one.

The holidays would be tough. Everyone said so. We girded ourselves. We didn't hide, we went to all the parties. We even entertained. Big time. Twenty-seven neighbors over for a Christmas party. We hosted a five-course dinner for six on New Year's Eve.

I made "Jessica" Christmas ornaments for Jessica's aunts. I bought all the six-inch purple-ball ornaments from two different Marshall Field's stores and had Caitlin use one of Jessica's signatures—actually, she never developed a classic handwriting, but rather printed—to use as a template for applying her name in gold glitter paint to the ornaments. I attached her last school picture to it on a purple ribbon, ensuring that for all those Christmases yet to come, everyone would pull out that ornament and with it their memories of Jess.

This is how far we had "progressed"—from barely being able to withstand the weight of the memories, to frantically trying to preserve them. I didn't want anyone to forget her. I didn't want to forget *anything*.

I asked Justin, Ben, and Caitlin to make me a book of "Jessica-isms," including all of her little sayings and idiosyncrasies, which were part of who she uniquely was. And, boy, did they load it up with that. Frankly, I was startled at first by the irreverence of it.

They even recorded the swear words she used ("shipsy hell biff"), the scatological references ("fudging baby hole"), and the mean things ("I don't love you!") Parts of it are darn-right funny, including "up your butt and around the corner."

But now I am forever grateful for having the whole picture. Not only did the book preserve memories of Jess, but it was another sign that my other children were surviving.

I still cry, though, when I think of how pure and unfiltered Jessica's love was. How many times did she grab me around the neck and say unabashedly, "I just love being with you"?

I know none of my other children would resent it or even doubt it when I say that no one will ever love us like that again.

Healing Dreams/Inner Voices

 Three years—Learning to live

I don't think there's any losing sight of grief.

You can't, really.

And you shouldn't, anyway.

You can never turn your back on it. In fact, the challenge is to keep it firmly in your sights, so you can safely back away, slowly.

If you're lucky, your field of vision eventually expands so that grief isn't the only thing you see.

Marriage—Surviving
As a Couple

The great irony of making it through the holidays that first year was that now we just had to get through the rest of our lives. In February, I cut out an article from the *New York Times*:

> The death of a child often shortens the life of the mother, a study by the Danish Epidemiology Science Center found. There was an increase in deaths during the first three years of bereavement, and most of the increase came from causes other than illness, like suicide or a car crash. There was also an increased risk among fathers, but a far smaller one.
>
> The risk was particularly acute among women whose children had died unexpectedly or from something other than illness. In the first three

years after the child's death, those mothers died at a rate almost four times as great as that of the mothers who had not lost a child.

After ten years, the effect on overall health began to show up, as deaths from natural causes among the bereaved mothers began to exceed those for mothers in the comparison group.

So, I would have to be vigilant for a lot longer than expected. It seemed wrong to have known both Jessica's beginning and her end. When your child dies, it's as if some cosmic taboo has been broken.

John and I became well-acquainted with the bittersweet. We were embarking on the pleasures of what we couldn't do when she was with us—travel abroad, going out on the spur of the moment. But that was accompanied by our painfully wistful memories of what was. It seemed as if happiness would forever have a hollow ring.

You read how couples often break up after the death of a child, so we felt threatened. We were each forever changed by Jessica's death, each confronted with the lonely task of binding our own wounds. We had to define who we were as parents without one of our children. We feared it might claim our lives as individuals. And our life together, as a couple.

And yet we understood that Jessica's death was somehow a part of our marriage story. If you survive it, suffering binds people together in a way that happiness simply does not.

You may always remember celebrating special events with a friend. But having that friend stand with you in your grief etches an indelible mark, creating runes that help you build the language of survival. That's what John and I were doing, learning this new language that began with unspeakable grief.

As a young woman, I categorized the men I knew into the Protectors (those who wanted to do things for me and to take care of me) and the Challengers (those who stood on their own, providing support as needed and who expected me to do likewise).

Luckily, I found John, who definitely was a Challenger. What he needed was a *strong* constant to stand with him, and I could do that. What I needed was a *steady* constant, and he could do that. More than four decades into the marriage, it's still working.

But of course, we couldn't know that in the beginning. John was hesitant about the idea of marriage. I didn't plan for it to be an ultimatum, but that's the way we still laughingly look back on my "proposal."

In 1974, after just over a year of dating, I was ready for one of two next steps: an advance *into* our relationship in the form of a more official declaration or an advance *out* of it, which was what New York and Columbia University offered. Receiving that one-or-the-other news at my flat in Detroit, John said he'd have to think about it. (Palm slap to forehead, but, OK . . . .)

He took off for the drive back to Ohio, and I honestly didn't know what he would decide. I sat down at my electric typewriter and wrote simply: "Waiting for the most important response of my life." I was very sure that this was the right time to create this juncture, however painful it might turn out to be.

Three hours later, the time it took him to arrive at his second-floor flat in Sidney, he called: "OK, let's do it." (I'm pretty sure it was true love, but we're still working on it, so I'll let you know.)

Absence truly did make our hearts grow fonder. During the course of my year in New York City—with John living in Ohio—we planned a wedding in yet another place: Detroit, for June 7, 1975.

We married relatively (our children say shockingly) young—he twenty-six, I twenty-three, within weeks of my graduation from Columbia. While I had spent the preceding year discovering one of the world's greatest cities, he was discovering rural Sidney, Ohio, as the farm editor (from Dee-troit) and a general assignment reporter in his first job out of college. When we married, we were literally coming from very different places.

Being part of an intimate, long-term relationship is a rare and precious experience. You learn it with your siblings, if you're lucky, but the experience is exalted with a life partner. Working with someone to build your corner of the world to make sure it is as resilient and beautiful as possible is the foundation of everything.

Across the globe, two people firmly grasping hands are what's holding up the whole world. Everywhere

Our wedding day.

you'll find people doing that hard work. My over-riding wish for my children is that they be among them, and I believe they are.

The secret is that love is both infinite and intimate—the only station in life where that duality exists. It's always within us, as potential, but not always with us, as realized experience. So, it is our perpetual quest to make love happen.

To be absolutely sure of being loved is the most valuable status in the world. Not forever, not for always, but on this day, in this moment. You and your lover must renew that commitment every day: I love you. Then you can fly and soar and risk and fail—but always with the knowledge that someone loves you. In that way, love makes you unkillable, no matter what you face.

This power exists in relationships beyond marriage, of course, including between parents and their children. Parents' love can make their offspring strong and steadfast, and courageous and brave. One of Jessica's therapists had called her a survivor in having emerged happy amid all she had to endure as a square peg trying to fit into a round hole.

In fact, she was unkillable; we, her family, made her so with our love.

John and I counseled engaged couples who were being married in our parish. We represented the "mixed" couple—although we raised our children Catholic, I remained a Protestant. In my experience, the god you grow up with is the god that stays with you.

Often the couples would ask us: What's the secret of a long, happy marriage?

Our answer: We only know what has worked for one couple, us, and if our knowledge were broader than that, we'd likely be selling it, not giving it away.

As a married person, you have a role in forming the mesh of a cohesive social order; you are a party to a civil contract, which is why you get a license. It starts with the bond you form with your partner and then expands to make your social network. There are no real supports for marriage in this society, so you have to be especially vigilant in preserving it. There's help when your marriage is in trouble but not before trouble starts, when you're simply participating in, maybe not even consciously maintaining, the relationship.

Life is so busy that married people often find themselves operating on autopilot. That's why it's important to make sure your marriage is also a covenant—a relationship that transcends the civil contract. You must agree to make your bond sacred, and only you can perform the incantations that make that happen.

John and I challenged ourselves to put a high value on the relationship by focusing on truth and trust. To make sure this pledge didn't become an empty platitude, we devised some real-world parameters: one partner could, at any time, decide to leave the relationship. But if that were the plan, they had to reveal that to their spouse before anyone else knew, even a new partner. A retreat from the relationship had to be done with respect—you had to bow out backwards, facing your partner.

That stipulation created a high hurdle; it may even have kept me from doing something stupid.

It's tempting to think there might be other people or situations that are better than the one you're in. And that may indeed be true, so you need to acknowledge that leaving the relationship is always a possibility. But that realization also requires that you keep holding on. Only you can sustain your relationship, so your marriage work has existential implications. The threatened impermanence of all our relationships makes them our most treasured possessions.

We need a spouse/partner who is a helpmate, which I bought into right away, and also an adversary, which I found a lot harder to appreciate. The whole concept of being a loving adversary—to challenge, to prod, to poke, to offer another viewpoint so that the best route eventually becomes clear—is a complicated business.

Often, it's exasperating, especially when your great idea isn't the one taken, even though it's so obviously pure and simple and right. And then there's the unsettling feeling that comes with knowing you have to give—sometimes a little, sometimes a lot—in the tug-of-war that leads to compromise and the best way forward.

(I'm reminded of the couple John interviewed on the occasion of their seventieth wedding anniversary. They had married as teenagers and people said it would never last.

"Looks like they were wrong," John said.

The woman looked over at her husband, who had been dozing throughout the interview, and retorted: "So far."

Point well-taken!)

John and I have each developed a fairly clear sense of our individual roles in preserving us and an urgent understanding that the only reason our relationship doesn't fall apart is that we're holding it together. In ways sometimes small and sometimes big, we renegotiate us almost every day. Are we still holding on? Are our grips tight enough? Do we even want to hold on? Why should we?

Our ability to do this was never more severely tested than when Jess died. We each needed to survive our own grief, but we had to survive each other's grief, as well. And our children's, because children are either de facto principals in your marriage during a crisis or they are collateral damage. Much was at stake.

The first step was participating in and enduring the wailing and the writhing, as the searing pain of our severance from Jess took hold. It is hard to say which is more difficult to bear in the onslaught of grief: your own pain or watching it subsume your spouse and children. In any case, the agony needs to happen.

But then someone—hopefully, you—is able to lift their head high enough to observe the carnage and shift their focus to the others. Did they survive? Are they able to stand?

After the first excruciating night, John and I were gradually able to do this through that mysterious, powerful mélange of faith, family, friends, human resilience, community. It was not a steady upward trajectory. We both regularly stumbled in despair, but we forced ourselves to keep our eyes on the horizon, where our children stood precariously.

For me surviving entailed bumping right up against the grief of my husband and children—listening to them, embracing them, holding them—but avoiding getting so close as to absorb the energy of their grief. (Think of those inflatable bubble balls that kids don to safely bump into each other on the playground.)

I was reserved in how much I gave the other grievers, including my husband. My first priority was saving myself, like the airline warning to make sure your oxygen mask is working before trying to help others in an emergency.

And I didn't always tell the truth about my pain, assuring myself that giving the other grievers what they needed—reassurance and support—was more beneficial than recounting my own pain. But sometimes I just needed to wail. And I needed to make sure my partner heard me.

John and I kept a wary, watchful eye on each other. We gave each other space to grieve in our own ways. John poured his feelings into his newspaper columns about our loss. I organized rituals: taking funeral flowers to Jess's grave, writing thank you notes to the senders, crafting Christmas ornaments so our family would always remember her, planning memorial funds in her honor.

From the beginning of our life without her, we regularly mentioned Jessica in conversations with our children, making sure the elephant in the room was acknowledged and thereby tamed.

All that, John and I could do. Our aching hope was that eventually we could break free from our commanding regimens and realize we had survived, still holding on, still together.

Our continuing tenacity hinges on the belief that there is a kind of grace in this relationship that cannot possibly exist in us as solitary individuals. That being responsible for someone else's fragile, vulnerable, treasured self is a task that sanctifies both parties. That this complex conjugal dance has meaning and purpose beyond the social institution. That it is, in fact, the most important work of a life.

Way back, when John and I were still in that tenuous phase of sizing each other up, Springsteen's

"Born to Run" lyrics spoke to my hopeful angst: his sad and lonely rider wanted to know if love was both wild . . . and real.

Nearly half a century later, it takes my breath away to say it's both.

Preach—Encounters of the Binding Kind

Holding on as part of an intimate relationship is never easy.

But ironically, the secret tool for maintaining your grip is knowing how to fight well. Conflict is a vital part of a relationship, but the combatants have to know the rules. You can fight any way you want if you don't really care about the end result. That's easy and very common.

If you really want to stay together, your fight has to produce two winners. (I know, it's not my favorite bit of reality, either.) You do that by listening to your partner until you really understand what they are saying. That deep listening can then lead to a compromise that ensures everyone's emotions and self-esteem are protected. In other words, you have to fight so no one is bloodied.

There is no one way to do this, and because restraint is the name of the game, my clean-fighting tips are based on strategic don'ts.

- Don't try to win. Otherwise, someone ends up losing, which means your relationship suffers. Instead find an outcome where both of you win. This is usually a compromise.

- Don't preach. When you get up on your high horse, you are no longer listening. *Listen.*

- Don't apply the silent treatment. Silence is not communication—it's a signal that you *don't* want to communicate.

- Don't change the subject. Communication is difficult; be brave.

- Don't fight from across a room, i.e., frying pan-hurling distance. Stay close (as long as neither of you is being physically abusive) and maintain eye contact. It's harder to be hurtful when you're touching each other.

- Don't make accusations. In fact, avoid the pronoun "you" altogether. Instead use "I," focusing on the way *you feel* about things, not what your partner did or did not do.

- Don't deliver an ultimatum, unless you're willing to live with the consequences. You foreclose discussion when you present one immutable option.

- Don't compare your partner to another member of their family. Keep the argument about the principals; everyone else is a distraction.

- Don't resort to name-calling. It's like swearing: It may make you feel better, but it doesn't advance the discussion.

- Don't bring up old incidents—another distraction from the real issue. Focus on the current conflict.

Even when you fight cleanly, one of you may still get hurt. If you are the one hurting, tell your partner, even though it may make you feel vulnerable and weak. Revealing your hurt lets your partner know that you trust them not to hurt you again.

If you are the one causing the hurt, sincerely engage in some crisis management: apologize, accept responsibility for your actions, and say what you'll do to avoid hurting your partner in the future. And mean every word of it.

Healing Dreams/Inner Voices

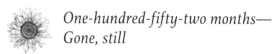 *One-hundred-fifty-two months—*
Gone, still

I dreamed that I was in bed, but it wasn't dark out. I saw Jess standing next to the window and lots of cars parked in our driveway.

I was so glad to see her! I told her that. And then, to confirm the experience, I took her hand and asked, "Where have you been?" I thought that if I could just hold on, I could keep her there.

She responded, "I've been living locally." And that made me chuckle because she *would* say something offbeat like that.

It was so real that I tried to tell John, but I couldn't because I was in that dream state.

Slowly, her hand in mine began to dissolve. And then she was gone.

I woke up. It wasn't real.

I wept.

The Duality—Loving, and Losing It

Like all of the wounded—which is to say, all of us—I have been casting about for a mantra to make sense of what has happened to me, to give it a purpose, to put it to use. I try to come up with the essence of what living is about, what it's for.

I settle on this: life is the struggle to be grateful for what happens to you—all of it. And then to act on that gratitude by bringing your generosity into the world.

Being grateful is a necessary first step, but it is very much an inward experience. You may feel gratitude, and that's great, but in terms of the larger world, so what? You have to act on that gratitude, and that action takes shape as generosity.

Finding gratitude amid loss is no doubt one of the toughest feats we perform. But it's crucial because there is no way to get to happiness unless we find a perspective that permits us to view what happens to us with gratitude.

Maybe not right away, not when we're still bleeding and scared. But later, when we're finished furiously shouting questions and demanding answers. When we're ready to simply open ourselves to something—often, desperately, anything—else.

That's when we can dare to start looking at the good that came before the loss and how much we gained from the experience of losing something precious—how much having it made us who we are, and how much losing it shapes who we will become.

When we can see that, gratitude starts coming into view and happiness begins taking shape. It may take a long time, so vigilance is required.

Finding your way to happiness is tricky because it's not transactional. It cannot be a goal—I *will* be happy—because happiness exists only as a byproduct of something else you're doing or experiencing.

We think happiness is something we achieve. But it's really there all the time. In some form, to some degree. The key to surviving is to position ourselves—however we can manage it, via religion, personal philosophy, simple hope—in such a way that we can see it. Enslaved people and Holocaust victims who were able to survive and make their way to happiness did so via gratitude. Read their stories; they're amazing.

The ability to appreciate sickness, death, pain, suffering, and despair empowers us to see beauty when others cannot—and to know gratitude in the most visceral way. And it's not only crucial in dealing with death; it's required in surviving all the other losses, too.

So how do you get to that first step, gratitude?

It starts with realizing that the good things that come your way—professionally and personally—are the result of not only hard work but luck. To survive and thrive, bowed but strong, is to be lucky. Very lucky.

When something good happens to me and someone says, "Congratulations, you *deserve* it," I cringe. Entitlement is dangerous in all its manifestations but especially when it takes shape as hubris, that overweening pride you see so much of these days.

You are not in control of everything, and that means that luck plays a major role in your experience. As talented as you may be, happenstance helps shape your life. And when you benefit from that luck, you should acknowledge it and be grateful, which in turn should infuse you with generosity toward others.

Life's superstars may not necessarily be more talented than you, just luckier. That's not making excuses, that's just reality. Youn Yuh-jung acknowledged this so eloquently when she won Best Supporting Actress at the 2021 Oscars for her role in *Minari*. Noting that her competition had included the accomplished (but Oscar-less) actress Glenn Close,

Youn, standing in the world spotlight, simply looked at Close and acknowledged: "I'm luckier than you."

See your good fortune as a kind of grace that has been bestowed on you, which you are responsible for sharing. This is especially true of the luck that may come as a result of your race and class. The follow-through is crucial because it assists the larger community's efforts to end the world's greatest burden: inequities in how human beings are allowed to thrive. Those inequities diminish all of us. So, make sure you put any good fortune you have to use in the world.

Recognizing the role of luck in life also allows you to appreciate its randomness. I think about the two urns Homer says stand on Zeus's doorstep: one with good fortune, the other with misfortune. Every mortal gets random quantities ... of both. The temptation is to assume that this applies to everyone except you, that somehow you can avoid the urn with the pain and suffering. This avoidance is what much of modern life is about, and it ascribes a controlling power to human beings that they simply do not possess.

My birthday falls on the traditional Memorial Day, May 30, so I learned early on about the good and bad urns. My birthday celebration often included a solemn visit to the cemetery to visit the graves of my maternal grandparents: bad, they died, but then a boisterous holiday parade—good, a triumphant spectacle in proud defiance of great loss. The good and the bad exist simultaneously.

Seven years after Jess died, Justin and his bride-to-be, Roxanne, sheepishly asked if it would be okay for them to marry on Jessica's birthday. Yes, we responded, bring on the joy!

In fact, Jess has been included in all of the subsequent sibling weddings. (And not at John's or my request.) Jess was listed on Ben and Sacha's wedding program as a bridesmaid; one groomsman walked down the aisle alone. At Caitlin and Tony's wedding, Jess was front-and-center as the prominent sunflower in the bride's bouquet and the wedding flowers.

When you are grateful, effectively channeling your losses and limitations, and generous, interacting with others in a way that helps build and solidify the world, you have seized your greatest power.

What does being generous in the world look like?

First, it doesn't start with money; that's way too narrow. At its most basic—its most powerful—generosity is simple kindness, being kind. Start there.

I think it also looks like forgiveness, so learn to forgive. This is hard because ultimately it has nothing to do with right or wrong, a dichotomy that can reduce the most complex issue to this or that, black or white, weak or strong.

Instead, acknowledge the transgression; there can be no denying it happened. But then determine if demonizing the transgressor brings you closer to the outcome you're looking for. Because if it doesn't, carrying around that resentment can be an onerous burden that lasts a lifetime.

Be generous with your spirit, your attention, your time, yourself.

Consider the generosity at work in making a meal for someone. In essence you are saying to your guest: this is all I've been able to gather, all I've worked so hard to prepare, all I can put before you to show how valuable you are to me.

(For me there is nothing more sublime than hosting dinner, experiencing the luscious joy of being together with friends and family around a table. The quote from Lord Byron that John and I put on our wedding invitation expressed so eloquently the compounding effect of sharing happiness: "All who joy would win must share it. Happiness was born a twin.")

And there's so much generosity in preparing for a guest's arrival: this is all the comfort I can assemble for you, everything I can think of to welcome you to the place in the world I call my home.

Simply greeting people warmly and fully is so generous. You're saying: I see you. I appreciate you. I want to make room for you in this moment.

Especially be generous in your relationships. Whenever possible, put the needs and wishes of the people you love before your own.

But even strangers can benefit from your generosity. Always be asking, What bit of light can I throw

The whole family at Caitlin and Tony's wedding: Grandsons Reid and Colin with their parents Justin and Roxanne, the groom and bride, John and me, Ben and Sacha, and the sunflower/Jess in Caitlin's bouquet. (2019)

onto the world with an act of compassion or forgiveness or simple kindness?

You can apply generosity in almost every human interaction you have. Think big when you do so. This is the great power of being generous—you can display it in the smallest of actions and it can result in disproportionately large impacts: simply offering a hand to someone who is struggling, complimenting the grocery store clerk on their packing, being patient, being a good listener.

At some point, you may even be able to put the needs and wishes of people you *don't* love above your own. That may be our ultimate state of grace.

Being thankful for all you have, the good and the bad, is hard because human beings don't want to look at the greatest limits we face, death and disease. I didn't, either.

But in my sixties, I started taking the first tentative steps in that direction. At my annual physical, I'd ask my doctor how I was likely to die, what he had read in the tea leaves of my blood work and current condition.

I could do that because I have been remarkably healthy, unthreatened as yet by the progress of my own mortality. My doctor, of course, had no idea what would ultimately befall me, so we settled on either heart disease or cancer, the leading causes of death in this country.

At first, recounting this exchange was amusing, reassuring even, as it became the source of joking with my friends. ("You actually asked your doctor what's going to kill you?!")

But then COVID-19 hit. Suddenly I was among the huge group of potentially compromised older adults. And once again I was confronted with limits, although this time I was better acquainted with their value. I understood the difference between realizing in a far-off sense that I would die at some point and knowing that because of the virus I had a good chance of dying much sooner.

Death is the ultimate limit, the unyielding given that makes life priceless, so time is the only commodity worth worrying about. Once you understand that, choices are much easier to make. How do you want to spend your limited time?

Dr. Atul Gawande crystallized the process for me in his book *Being Mortal: Medicine and What Matters in the End*. He was blunt: Our bodies allow us to be in the world, but they are designed to ultimately fail.

Acknowledging our mortality means that our well-being is defined by the reasons we want to be alive. The challenge is to identify those reasons and never lose sight of them, especially as we face illness and death.

That requires digging down to the moment-to-moment essence of our lives. What is most important to us in those moments? And how do we hold on to it?

Once you identify the prized essential elements

of your life, hope replaces fear. You're empowered to live the life you want, right up to the end. Gawande laid out the process:

- Understand your situation and the potential outcomes. Describe the scenarios you face with as much realistic detail as you can muster.
- Determine what trade-offs you are willing to make—or not—to live your best life, right up until the end.
- Then, with those parameters in mind, decide how to proceed.

We're so hard-wired by the culture to look at the longer term that this intimate step into the moment is difficult. But facing life on your own terms requires that you know what your terms are.

I discovered that when confronted with whether to donate my daughter's organs. I'm forever grateful for having considered organ donation before Jessica died. It allowed me to act with resolve when faced with the unfathomable.

By chance, or astounding prescience, the year before COVID-19 hit I started what I called the Mortality Club with three friends. Our plan was to create our individual advance directives, a guideline for our families and doctors regarding how we wanted to live our lives to the very end, including being present at our own deaths.

I was eager to do this because I wanted to be thankful for my life—and by my definition that meant being happy with my life—right through to my dying day. Depending on the circumstances, I might need an advance directive so my family could help me do that.

Perhaps most difficult of all, this required talking with them about my demise. (Note to self: It's hard being you, even at the end.)

We Mortality Club members—we called ourselves Mortals—researched aspects of the end-of-life process that interested us in particular. One friend, Mortal 67, looked into the quality-of-life consequences of certain life-saving options, such as CPR and ventilators. Mortal 60 researched work/life choices and how those choices would hold up in the face of debilitating illness.

I explored how we face our medical challenges in an intentional way, avoiding extraordinary measures that extend our lives but not our well-being. That dichotomy was one I hadn't really considered, and it became more complicated as I continued to follow Steve Gleason on social media, and he continued to defy the boundaries I imagined I'd erect if my abilities were severely compromised.

Steve showed me that limited abilities don't necessarily mean a limited life when you have the right supports. And those supports are crucial, so Steve has established the nonprofit Team Gleason to deliver innovative technology and equipment to empower and improve the life experience of people with ALS. Team Gleason has provided more than $20 million in adventure, technology, equipment, and care services to more than 20,000 people.

I've been committed to demonstrating that limits to my speaking ability don't limit my life, but Steve has taken it far beyond that, to encompass essentially his entire physical interaction with the world.

What researcher Peter Ubel had found stuck with me: "By being forced to abandon normal day-to-day activities, people begin to think seriously about what pursuits will fill their lives with the greatest sense of meaning and purpose."

Steve had absolutely done that with his intense focus on his family and creating the Team Gleason foundation. (See his resoluteness at work in the 2016 film *Gleason*.)

When you know there's a finite end, you focus on your passions. As Ubel noted: "I have slowly come to believe that nothing is more detrimental to a well-lived life than having gobs of time."

Wow, so our incessant wish for more time may actually undermine our attempts to make a mark on the world.

Ubel concluded: "I hope to live my life with enough sense of imminent death to focus my energy on pursuing meaningful goals."

The messages Steve and Ubel were relaying at once intrigued, confounded, and overwhelmed me. Disability, disabling conditions, limits, and losses can help people reset their priorities. By altering their goals to their new circumstances, people adjust what brings them joy, so that their limits have no effect on their happiness. Resilient people just find another way to be happy.

But are we strong enough to do that? Am I strong enough to do that?

And at what point is there strength in letting go?

The mean survival time with ALS is two to five years, according to the ALS Foundation. Only about 10 percent of people with ALS live more than 10 years; 5 percent live 20 years or longer. Steve was diagnosed in 2011.

But not everyone has Steve's resources and support network. The vast majority of people with the disease (90-95 percent) decline living with the tracheal tube and mechanical ventilation that Steve chose.

All of that, and more, is why end-of-life issues are so difficult.

There was much to consider as we Mortality Club members persevered with our task, presenting our findings and thoughts, and discussing them late into the day.

Then we each began filling out Aging with Dignity's "Five Wishes" document, an easy-to-use legal advance directive that helps you consider and record how you want to be cared for at the end of your life. It's the most popular living will in the country, with more than thirty-five million copies in circulation. Many doctors distribute it free of charge

in their offices, or you can buy it at www.FiveWishes.
org. It allows you to specify:

1. The person you want to make care decisions
    for you when you cannot.
2. The kind of medical treatment you want or
    don't want.
3. How comfortable you want to be.
4. How you want people to treat you.
5. What you want your loved ones to know.

We Mortality Club members understand that
our wishes could change, so we remain on standby
for the next meeting. We know our mortality will
increasingly demand our attention.

Dr. Francis Collins, then director of the National
Human Genome Research Institute, spoke at the
University of Michigan when I was there on my fellowship in 2001. The research institute was close to
completing the mapping of the human genome, the
building blocks of human life, which would have
implications for improving our understanding of
health and disease.

Collins's focus as a physician-geneticist included
the legal and ethical issues involved in manipulating
genes, which were a key part of my studies that year.
I was star-struck.

Collins is a religious man. He says faith provides

a way to wrestle with the major questions of life, not the least of which is our mortality, and notes that religious experiences make it easier for us to find happiness and emotional resilience. Many studies have found religion to be a consistent predictor of happiness.

For Collins, faith necessarily intersects with science because he believes we are more than atoms and molecules.

I believe that, too. But it was literature, not religion per se, that crystallized my understanding of just how sacred our experience of the world can be. And how we should always be looking for evidence of its sanctity.

An audio version of Truman Capote's short story "A Christmas Memory" always came with us when John and I took the kids to Detroit for the family Christmas Eve party. Near the end of the story, the older woman revels in the joy of spending Christmas Day with her young nephew, Buddy, flying kites they had made for each other. The gifts are all they could afford, but they are glorious. As she and Buddy watch their kites soar—and with what I imagine is a rapturous sense of gratitude (for Buddy's gift to her) and generosity (in her gift to Buddy)—she triumphantly proclaims that she'd be satisfied to die with just the memory of that moment in her eyes.

I look for those moments, and I recognize their blessedness.

My daughter, Caitlin, understands—and often

even indulges—this existential bent of mine. And although she doesn't quite acknowledge it (she's a facts-based journalist, after all), I think she's developing her own version. She's the first to buy sunflowers around the time of Jessica's death and send me photos of them. The sunflower is our shared symbol of resilience; we both survived.

In fact, we *all* survived, so sunflowers make their way into family wedding flowers and treasured gifts that are bestowed on me. My daughters-in-law and son-in-law—who know Jess only through their spouses—also participate. Their willingness to do so acknowledges and honors the life our family led before they were part of us. It is a very generous act.

I work hard to recognize and give thanks for these and all the other "kites" I've received, especially the gifts that are family and friends, who have stood with me in the wind. . . .

Preach—Enumerating Infinite Messages

I come back to the talisman that poet Mark Strand sought to give his own Jessica. Among the items he mentioned was a sheet of paper, something to help guide his daughter even when they were no longer in the world together. I was looking for that, too.

Of course, I never imagined my daughter would be the one going away first. Maybe that jarring of the natural order is why it has taken me so long to get this down. I've been searching for ways to stay close to Jess amid the darkness that is death.

But by resolutely—sometimes, fearfully—walking through that darkness and then inscribing lessons learned on my own sheet of paper, I have managed to survive.

Now I'm passing that sheet of paper on for my remaining children to carry in the dark when I am away.

1. Struggle to learn from losses and limits.

To be happy you must learn to live with loss. This is the key to everything—every thing. I know, it seems weird, being happy via what makes you unhappy.

So let me explain: Loss and limits provide us with a sense of proportion, which is crucial to appreciating and being grateful for anything. There is no such thing as happiness in a vacuum. In the broadest sense, we appreciate life because we know we will die, and we value health because we know illness is all around. Having losses and limits as counterpoints is crucial because they allow happiness to shine brighter in contrast.

No matter what happens to you—the good and the bad are inevitable—what's important is to have the focus to live life with intention, and the courage to live it with intensity. The degree to which you approach life with those two goals in mind—intensity and intention—is the degree to which your aspirations will match your accomplishments. To keep your focus, do something each day that moves you toward your goals. Go for it; the world needs what you can do.

2. Find a place for loss and limits.

Losses have more than twice the psychological impact as equivalent gains, research shows. But you must unravel how those losses and limits fit into your life. You must fashion a life that includes that negative space.

Loss changes you, but you get to decide how. Some say loss makes you brave, but bravery never gets put in your lap—here's a loss, now you're brave. You have to *be* brave. Loss doesn't define your life so much as help you shape it, which means it can be empowering. There is value in limits.

But watch out for how society sets limits for people. As a person who stutters, I was advised to do silent work. But our limits are not a set of pathologies—they are part of our personal stories, which only we can write. Society gives our limits one context, but we must fight like hell to find our own meaning because society's expectations are often pitifully skewed.

Incorporating losses and limits into your life will make you hyper-aware that the whole world is similarly struggling. Recognize the stunning ubiquity of loss, which will teach you to be kind. The value of this process cannot be overstated.

3. Be grateful. More importantly, be generous.

They say gratefulness is the ideal state, but it's actually generosity. Gratitude is your internal monologue; generosity is your gratefulness at work in the world.

Be generous with your money but also with your spirit, your attention, your time, your self. Especially be generous in your relationships—focus on what others need from you.

To be generous you have to acknowledge the role of luck in your life. Only then can you experience the deepest sense of gratitude, which is the catalyst for generosity. Watch out for people who credit themselves for their good fortune; hubris is dangerous.

Always seek to pass along your good fortune in whatever proportion it comes to you. As George Eliot wrote in *Middlemarch,* "What do we live for, if not to make life less difficult for each other?"

Concentrate on your responsibility to the world and your all-important rights will find their place. Don't go looking for accolades, which are merely a distraction from your appointed task. Instead, work to give the world what it needs, what only you can provide.

At its most basic, your gift is simply your kindness at work in the world. Everyone is pained in some way and, ironically, the pained are often those who are hurting others, maybe even you. That alone is worth noting, since that pain plays out in human relationships all the time, and you will want to understand what you're dealing with. Whenever possible, be kind, but do not sacrifice yourself.

4. Determine what constitutes "enough."

Learn to measure and know the elusive concept of Just Enough. You need to know: What do I *want*? What do I *need*? And then you have to understand the difference between them, to ensure your wants are not infinite.

Beware of mis-wanting, erroneously believing that attaining something will make you happy; it's too easy to end up wanting the wrong things. It turns out happiness is not directly attainable; it is always a byproduct. We overestimate the intensity and duration of our emotional reactions to both good and bad, research shows. Learn to moderate your expectations for both happiness and grief, since neither is likely to be as powerful and enduring as you think.

People are not good at choosing, often because we are always looking to make sure we get the most out of our choices. But considering opportunity costs—fearing missing out on something else because of a particular choice you make—can tyrannize you. Instead know when to choose the good enough. Embrace the choices you have within the limits you're dealt. You need just enough power to act on your aspirations, so you can be You. Everyone should have that ability, and we all share the responsibility to ensure everyone does.

5. Know the interconnectedness of the world.

There is value in the way things fit together, in the interconnectedness of things. The world seems particularly confused right now about how things fit together, although maybe this is always the human condition. We don't have a blueprint that reflects our shared understanding of how the world is connected. So, the choices our leaders and sometimes we ourselves make are often weak in their isolation. And there is no willingness to adjust them.

Despite that frustration, it's your responsibility to participate. I hope you will be ever at work connecting the world. It needs you.

6. Know humility; understand weakness.

Your opinion is often not nearly as important as you assume. Always consider what the person requesting it really needs; make sure you're really listening. Many times, they won't be asking for your objectivity but for your support and affirmation. Unless that would ultimately be harmful, you should supply it. Truth-telling is overrated when it satisfies the needs of the teller (in her self-righteousness), not those of the seeker. Examine your own motivations.

Always keep in mind how vulnerable people are, even—perhaps, especially—those making life miserable for you. We tend to give hurtful people credit for much more power than they actually have.

Mostly, they're afraid. (The portion of bad behavior I attribute to foolishness has consistently declined over the years. Fear may be the world's greatest plague.)

You will have to look deeply to determine which weakness someone is operating from. But once you do, calm, reasoned responses are much easier.

7. Always be listening.

. . . to the world, nature, your friends, your enemies, your heart. This means you must be silent more often than you think—most of the time. You have to be tuned in to learn and grow as a human being, and you must be committed to the task. (You likely experience this as well, but I can't tell you how often the person I'm talking to seems to consider my comments merely a prelude to what they want to say, instead of actually hearing me and responding to what I said.)

You simply listening is the gift. Not you as the storyteller or the savior with the right answer, both of which are powerful enticements to speak. Instead, just listen, make sure you understand what you've heard, and then apply critical thinking to see if it resonates in your heart and mind. At that point, you've earned the right to be an actor in the world. I know you'll be good at it.

8. Know your purpose in the world:

- Be whatever you want, but be a good one. (A quote attributed to many; I choose Abraham Lincoln.)

- Take chances! Make mistakes! Get messy! (Definitely and definitively, a quote from Ms. Frizzle.)

- Work to build the common good.

- Know that you carry a piece of what the world needs and is waiting for you to apply.

- Leverage your most valuable power—the ability to empower others. Start by simply telling someone they're doing a good job; it can be transformative.

- Hone your ability to notice miracles; otherwise, you'll never see them. Make it a point to recognize one every day. They'll start to add up.

9. Finally, belong...

- To a person (know at least one person intimately);
- To a tribe (participate in a family, a cause, a religion, a profession); and
- To a place (find somewhere that calls you to be present).

Belong, so that in being with that person, or with that tribe, or in that place you will know the great comfort of coming home.

Making Meaning

Here is one last story, "Recovering," from my journal. It's written with loving thankfulness for John Schneider, my partner through journeys of varying depths and many times over, good and bad, and still we stand, together, holding on.

This night, September 7, 2018, brought an amazing revelation. And I knew we were destined to live it, even as I took my role in the events. (Be woke to your life and the miracles around you.) The scene is the cove on Lake Huron where our cottage sits. (Belong to a place that calls you.)

The wind had temporarily died on the big lake and we were taking a walk before dinner. We passed George's place and the spot where Jessica died, down to the point on the cove where the relentless waves had uncovered a treasure—a big pudding-stone, creamy quartzite with chunks of red jasper.

It was heavy, but we had a plan: We would take turns carrying it.

We didn't get very far. It was much heavier than even our desire to possess it could move. Still, we had nudged it far enough to make it ours, away from the dog tracks and footprints on the beach, isolated in our eyes from the rest of the shoreline.

We left it there, plotting our return. We'd move it by kayak. Maybe, just maybe, we could float a rock that seemed bigger than us.

After dinner the lake started roiling and we got anxious to recover what we were already calling "our" rock. We had to paddle into the mounting waves, and they slapped us. We hugged the shore but kept the destination in sight. As only we knew, the rock lay just down from the point, near the beached log.

Landing was tricky. Luckily the lake hadn't turned over and the water was still warm as we waded in to pull the kayak to shore. We struggled to get the rock into the kayak, turning it on its side in the sand, careful not to let in the persistent waves. Then, summoning our dual strength, we pushed the big rock in with a tremendous shove. Amazing!

Now, would the kayak float?

We fumbled to get ourselves into the kayak. The hulking stone seemed to resist accommodating us, requiring some contortions. John adjusted his seat to give the rock wide berth; I pulled my knees up to my chin.

The kayak rocked precariously with our collective weight, and we held our breath until slowly, slowly, it steadied amid the waves. For a moment we sat silently, wide-eyed at the wonder of it all.

Then we pushed off. Somehow, we were floating.

We could ride with the waves this time, although we regularly found ourselves in deep water if we weren't careful. The wind and waves whipped the three of us—we two and our treasure—when the kayak veered toward open water.

We doubled down: Keep paddling, keep paddling. The motion became our mantra.

Then, looking up from the surrounding white-caps, we realized our beach was close, closer than we thought. How lucky to have made the recovery when we did! We pulled the kayak onto shore, as far as we could, and with a heave dumped our treasure on the beach for all to admire.

High-fives all around.

A light shined in the kitchen window as we hurried into the cottage. (We must have forgotten to turn it off.) We put on dry clothes, grabbed a blanket and sat silently, looking out at the waves and marveling at our luck: To be home with our treasure, drinking bourbon and tequila, triumphant.

Together.

Safe.

Happy.

Thank you. Thank you.

One Last Healing Dream

 Not long ago

I dreamed John and I were in a restaurant with the Knight-Wallace journalism fellows, and I needed to get something from the car. (A similar incident happened in Buenos Aires with the fellows, when John and I were trying to find an internet cafe to call our kids while the others were settling in at a nearby restaurant.)

I went out one side of the building and couldn't see the car, so I turned the corner and went down a side street where there was a lot of construction at the curb.

The car was there and Jess was in it, holding the book I was looking for. Jess was very excited about the book, and I was thrilled to see her so happy.

I looked at the book—it was written by me! I was on the cover in a black top, smoking a cigarette, in a very large, tight shot. (I cringed at the smoking, but

figured the journalism fellows wouldn't disapprove.)
I stood there—on the street, with the book—as the
dream dissolved.

Slowly waking, I wondered where Jess had disappeared to in the dream. I had last seen her as she got
out of the car, tightly grasping the book. The precise
hand-off hadn't been recorded in my dreaming brain.

But now I know.

The transfer has finally happened. *This* is the book.

Mother and child are forever tethered. So when Jess
fell into that bottomless chasm that is death, it was
treacherous for me. Would the rope connecting us
prove too short for the descent? Would I be pulled in
after her?

Many times I felt the menacing tug. Many times I
wanted to surrender to it.

But I have been able to maintain my ground, and the
tether has created the narrative line I've been seeking
for so long. All of the disparate, loose elements of my
existence have been pulled taut.

Hopefully, that tether will prove useful to someone else. Maybe my children. Maybe you.

In any case, it has allowed me to live.

And it has allowed Jessica to live on.

Jess and me.

Acknowledgments

Many thanks to my tribe of family and friends, who encouraged me to speak to the world, especially:

- Jennifer Carroll, who read two essays I brought to her one cold January afternoon in northern Michigan and said they were worth turning into something more.

- Sarah Kellogg, who lived through some of these events and painfully relived them as my first editor.

- My daughter, Caitlin Schneider, who cried with me when tears were unwanted but vital.

- Karen Stock, who read through early drafts, made thoughtful suggestions, and continues as my right-hand woman.

- Judy Winter, who showed the way with her book.

- Holly Sasso, who read early drafts and will be the next to follow with her own book.

- Kathy Hoffman and Dave Waymire for helping me shine in this new role.

- *Writer's Digest* agents who pointed out what my almost-there first chapter lacked.

- Anne Stanton, Mission Point Press editor, and Heather Shaw, designer, who worked on this project as if it were their own.

- The late great Kelly Rossman-McKinney, who showed me the power of filling up a room with myself, instead of desperately trying to make an impression by not standing out.

- Michel Varisco Gleason, Judith Ursitti, and all the world's caregivers, for showing us what true grit is.

About the Author

SHARON EMERY has always had a penchant for communicating, but speaking is a struggle because her voice includes a stutter. Sometimes, a bad one. So writing became her voice. Sharon forged a career in journalism, public relations and teaching, but she still stutters. Luckily, it has taught her a lot about surviving life. Today, when not traveling to see her far-flung children, she and her husband live in Michigan—on twelve acres near Lansing and on Lake Huron near Cheboygan. She is happy.

Made in the USA
Monee, IL
23 May 2023

34394053R00166